Mandala Coloring Book for Adults and Children

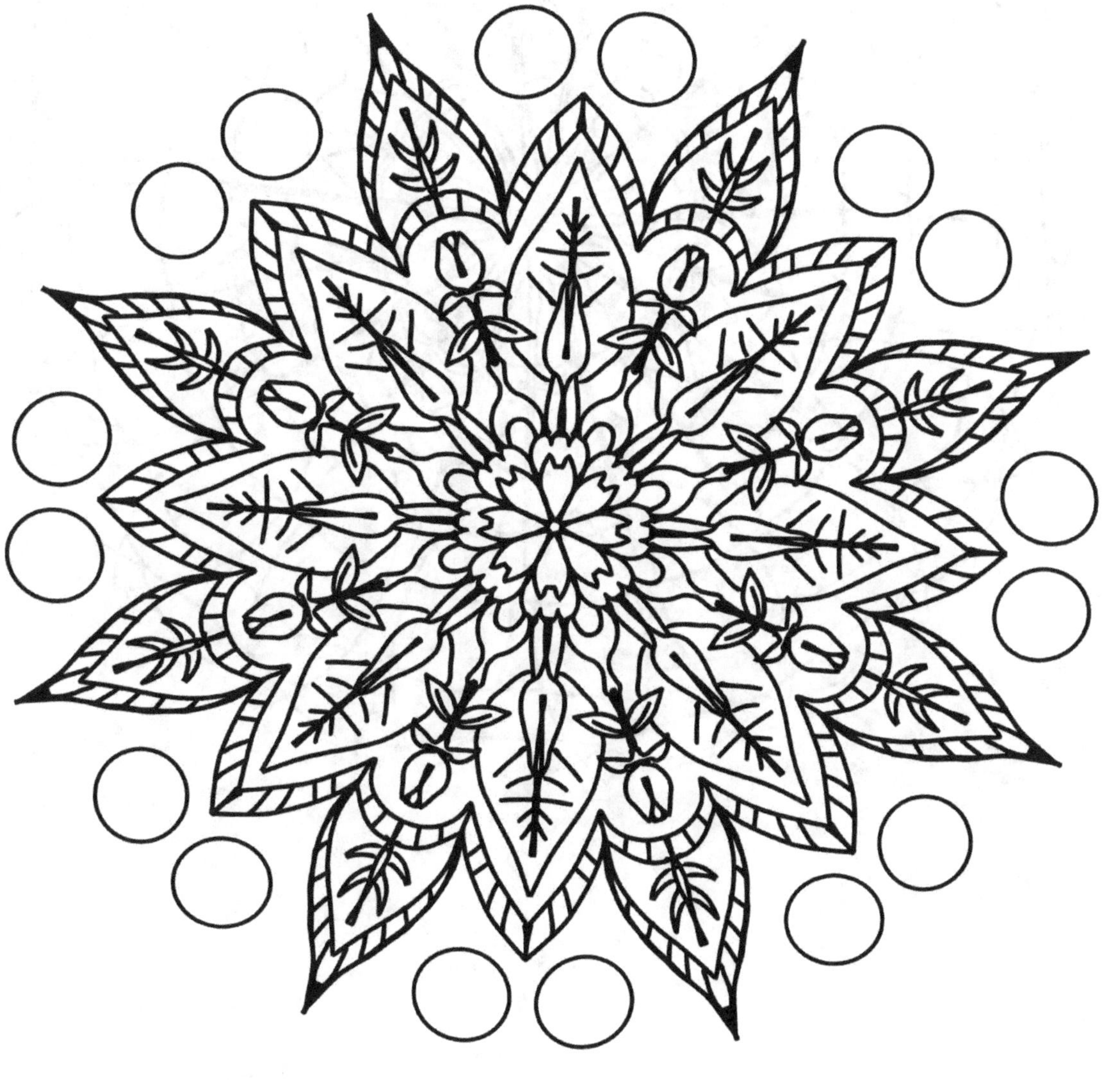

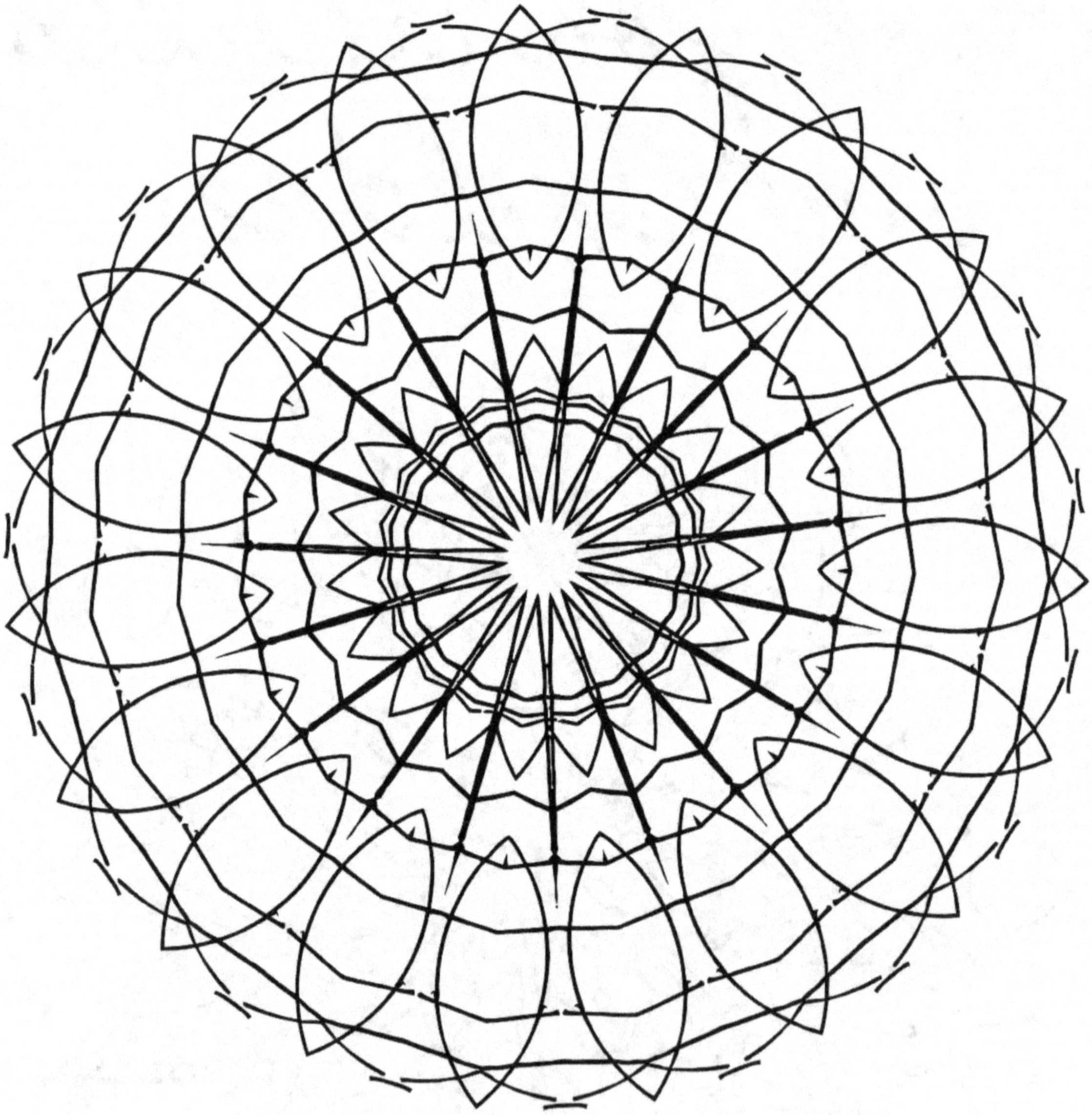

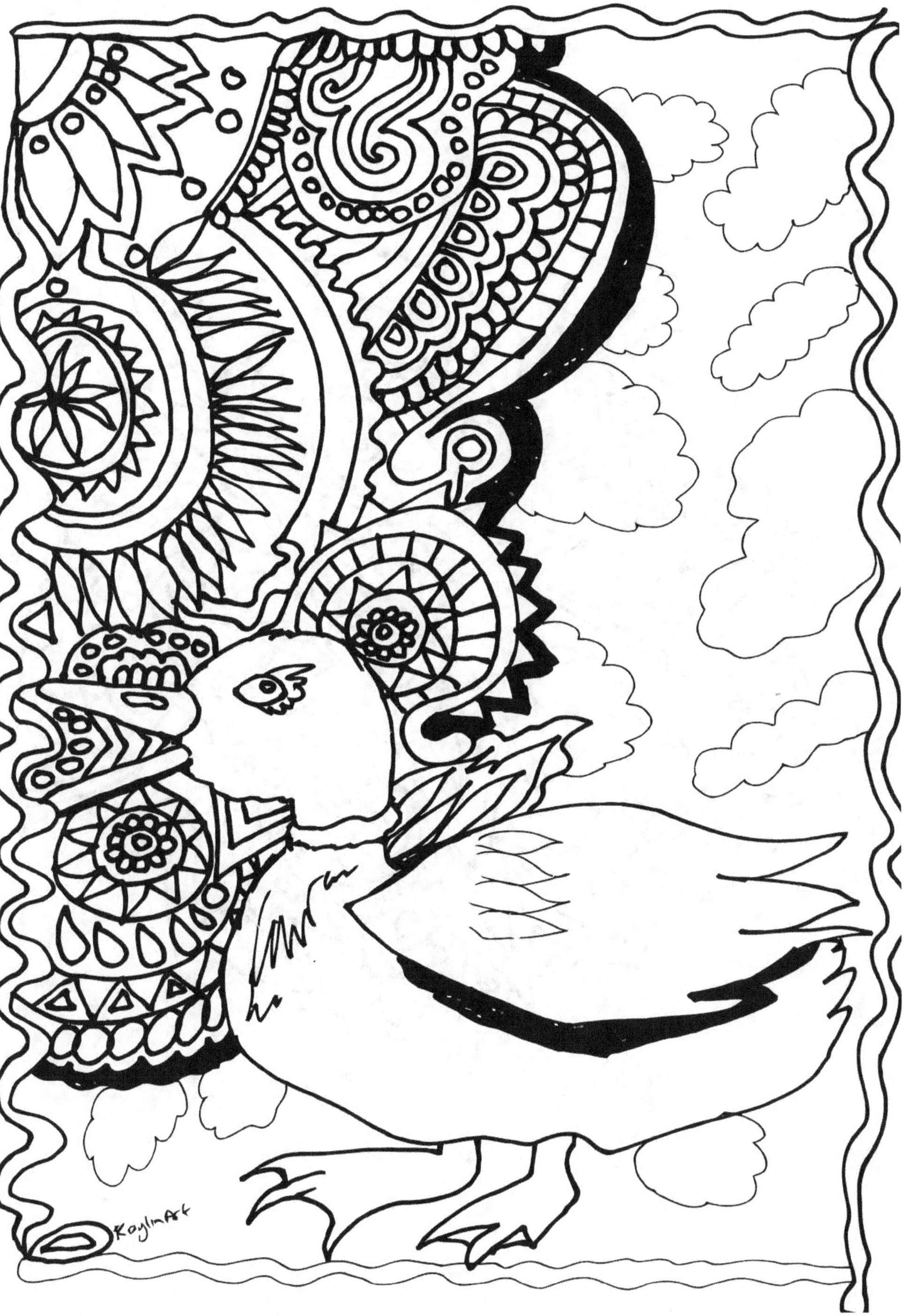
KaylinArt

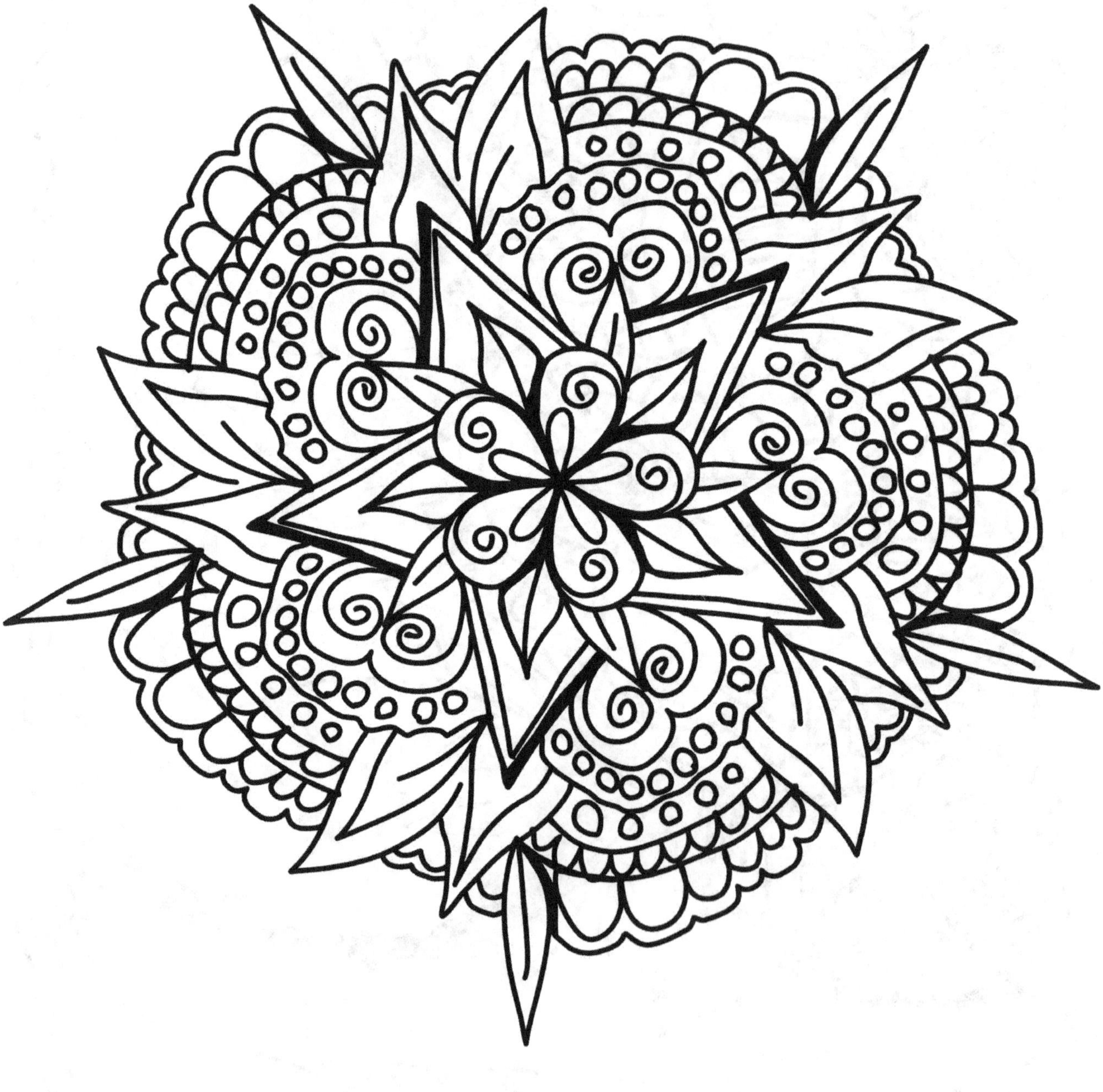

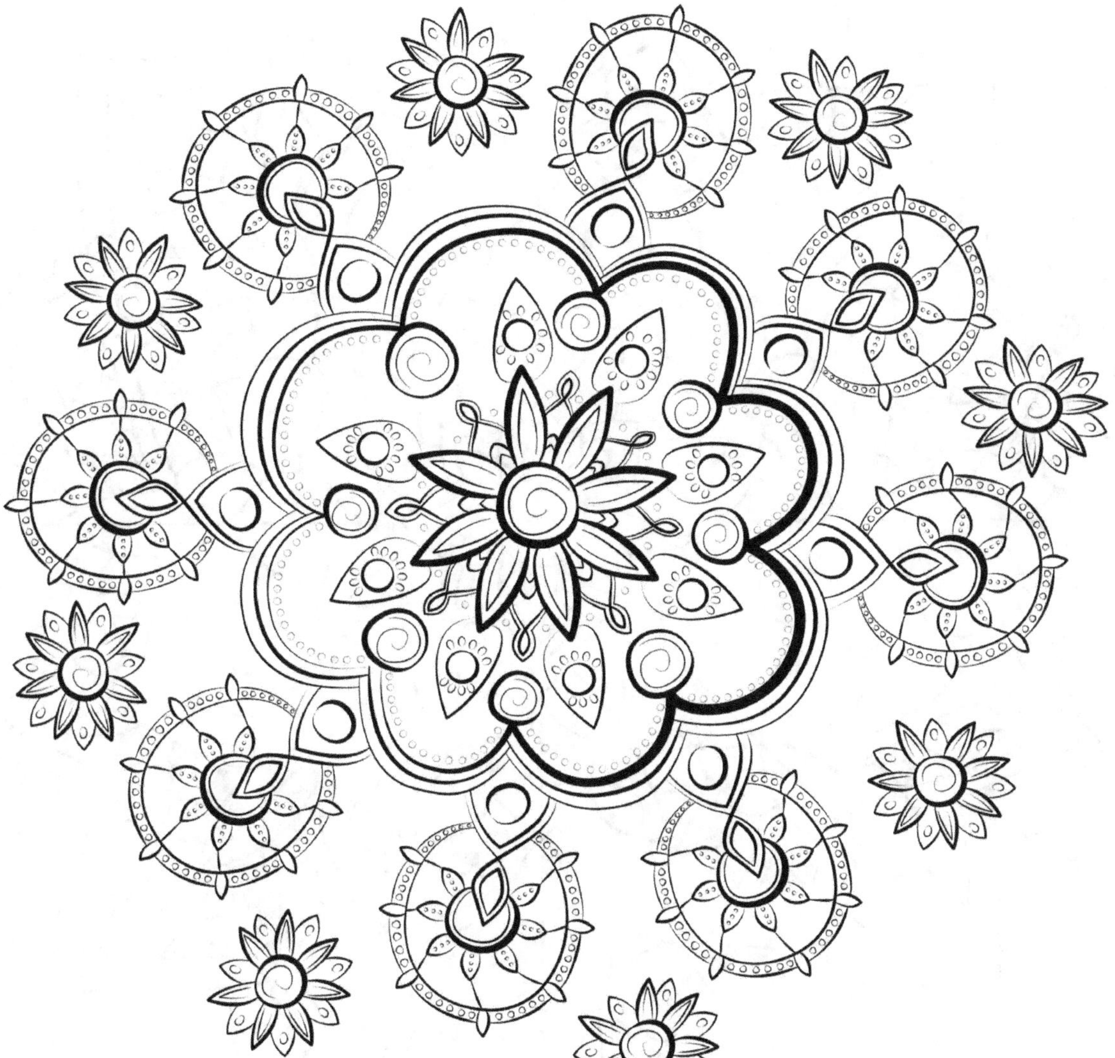

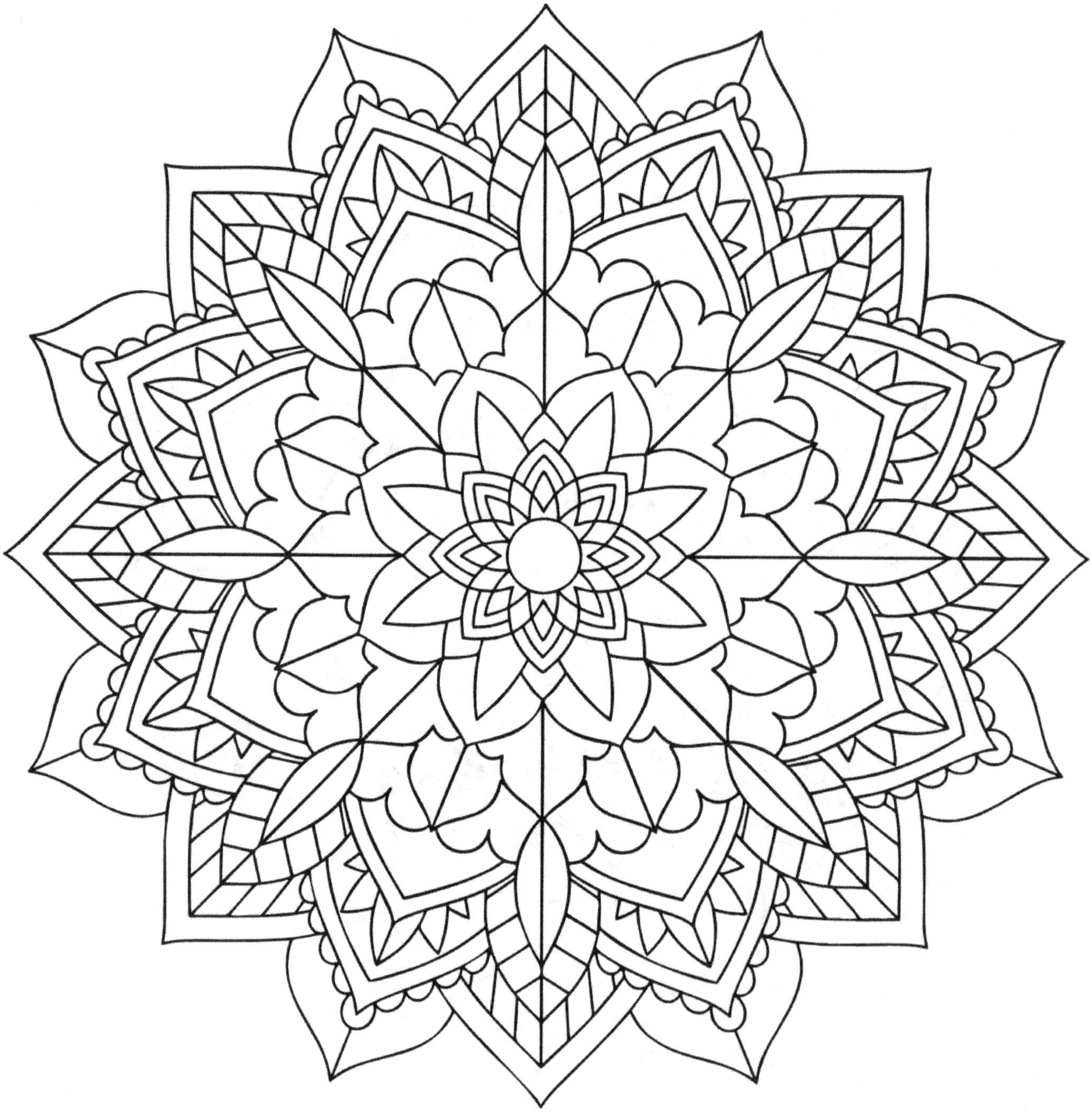

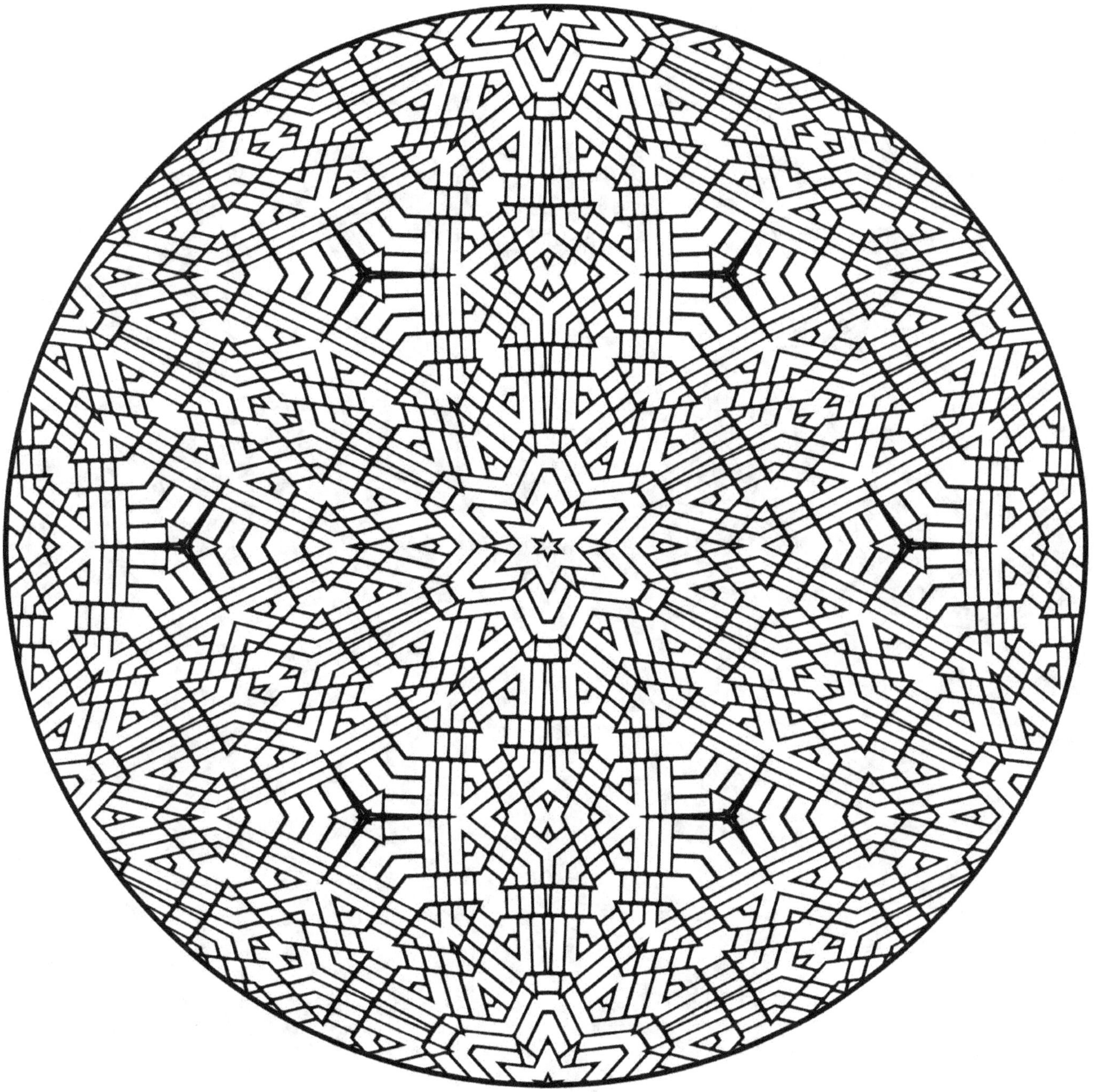

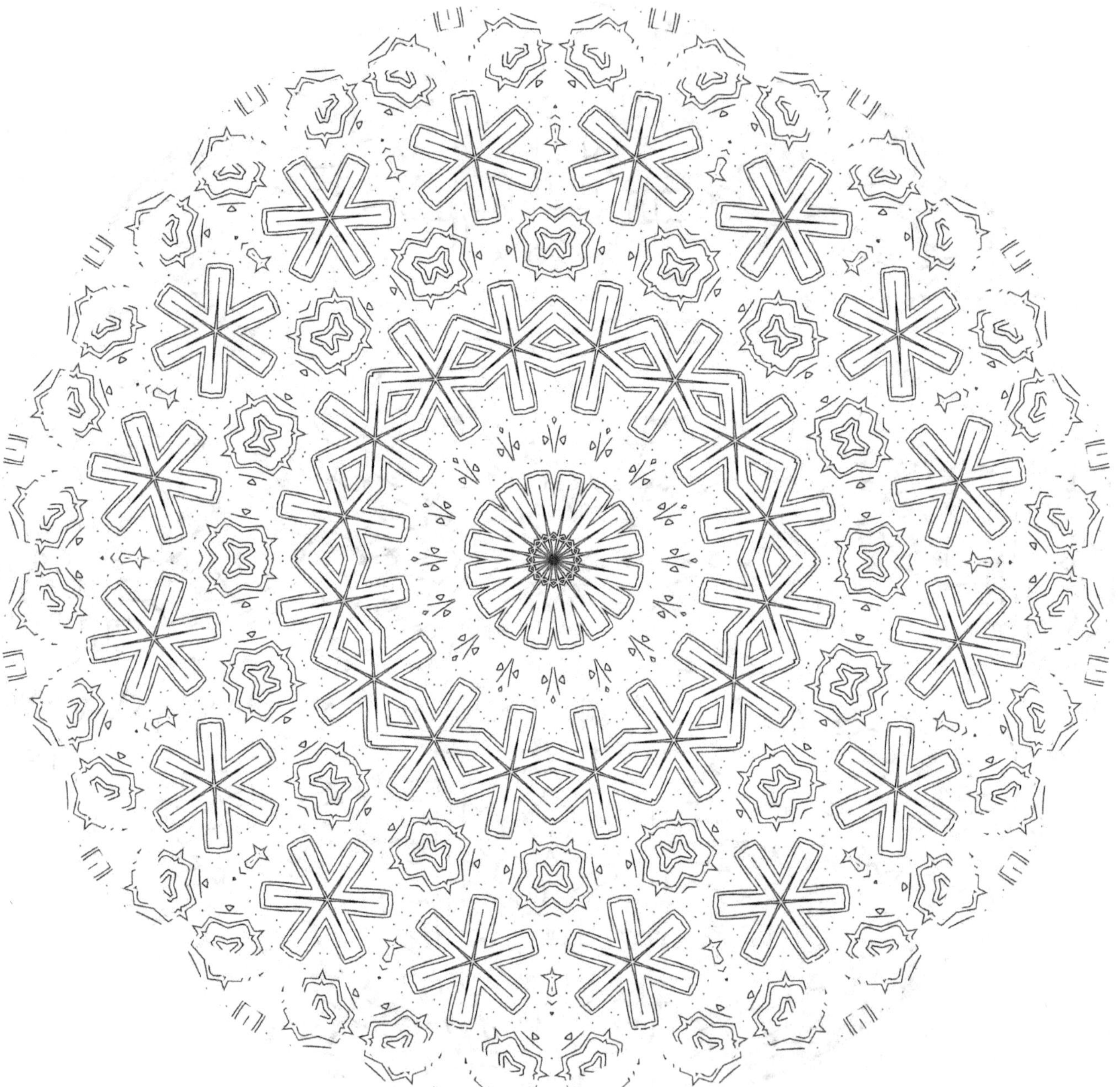

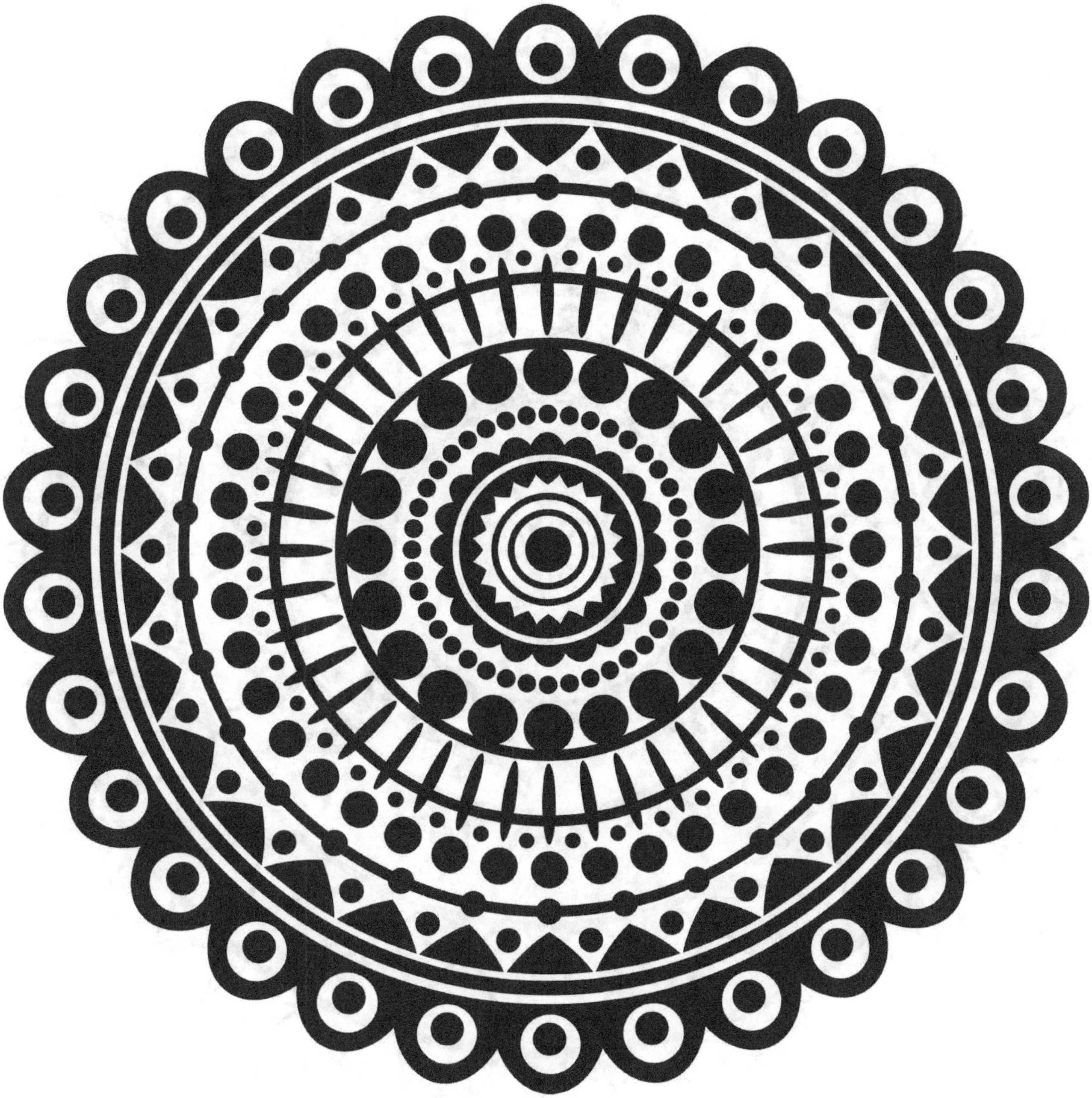

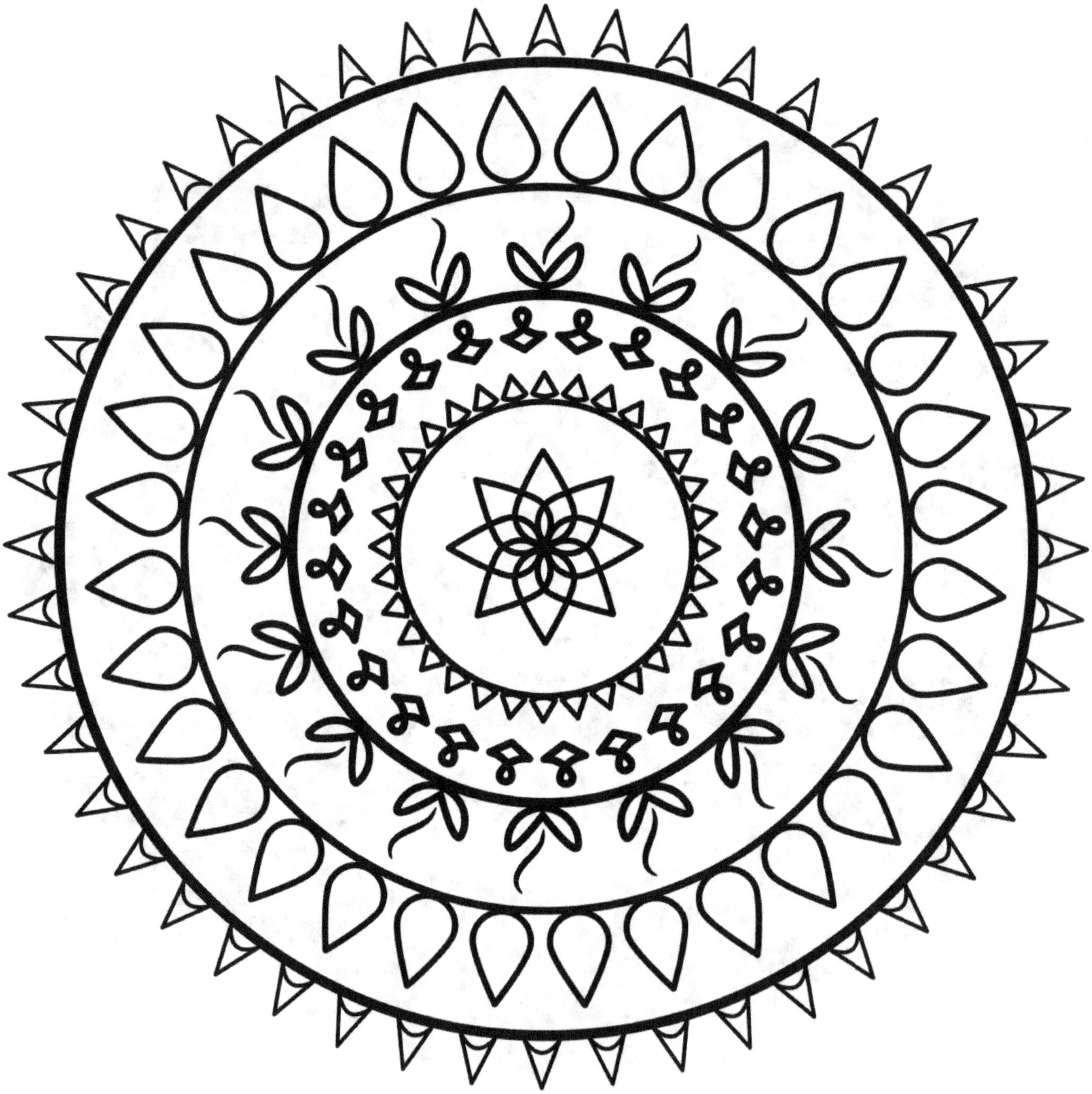

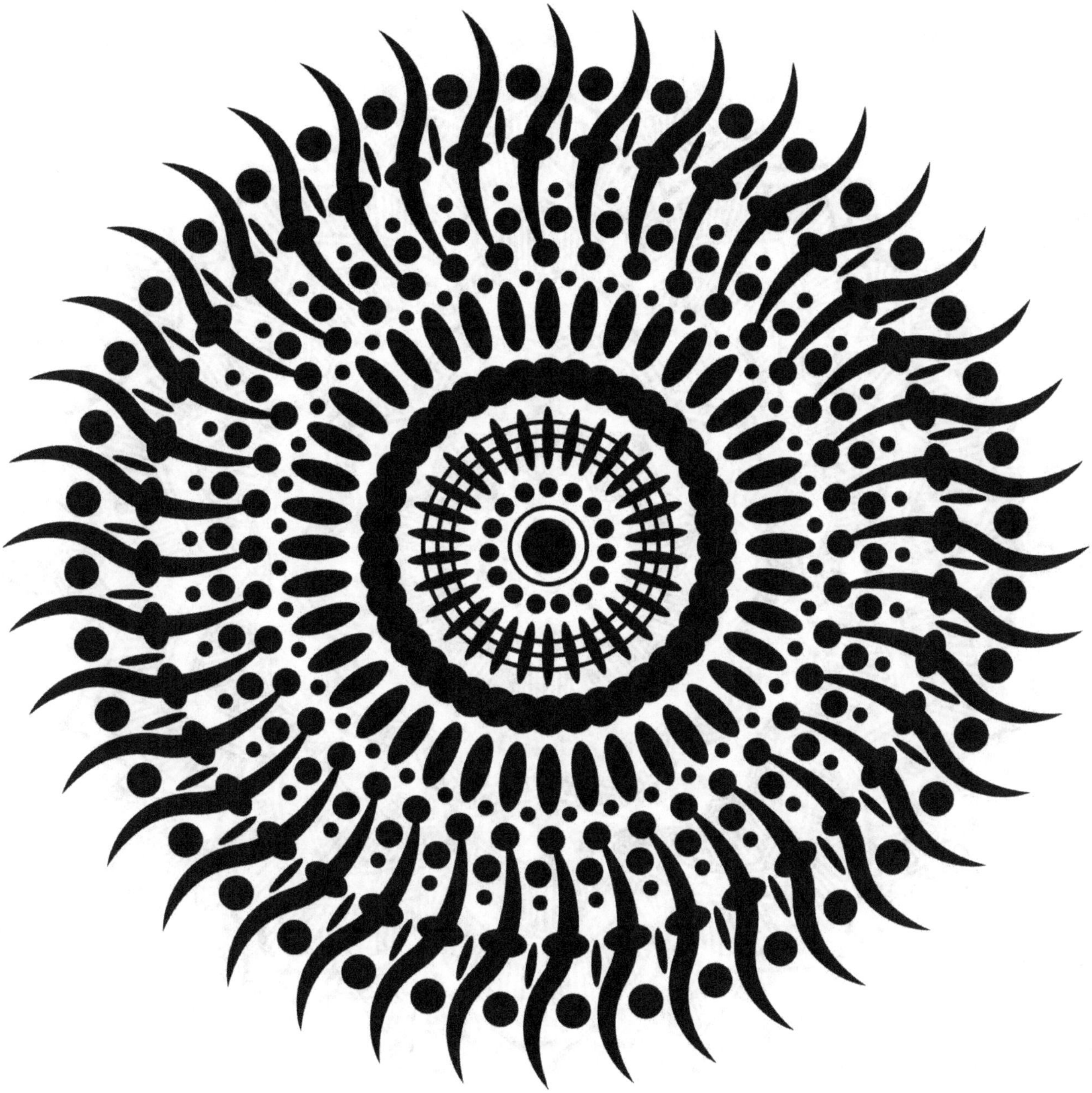

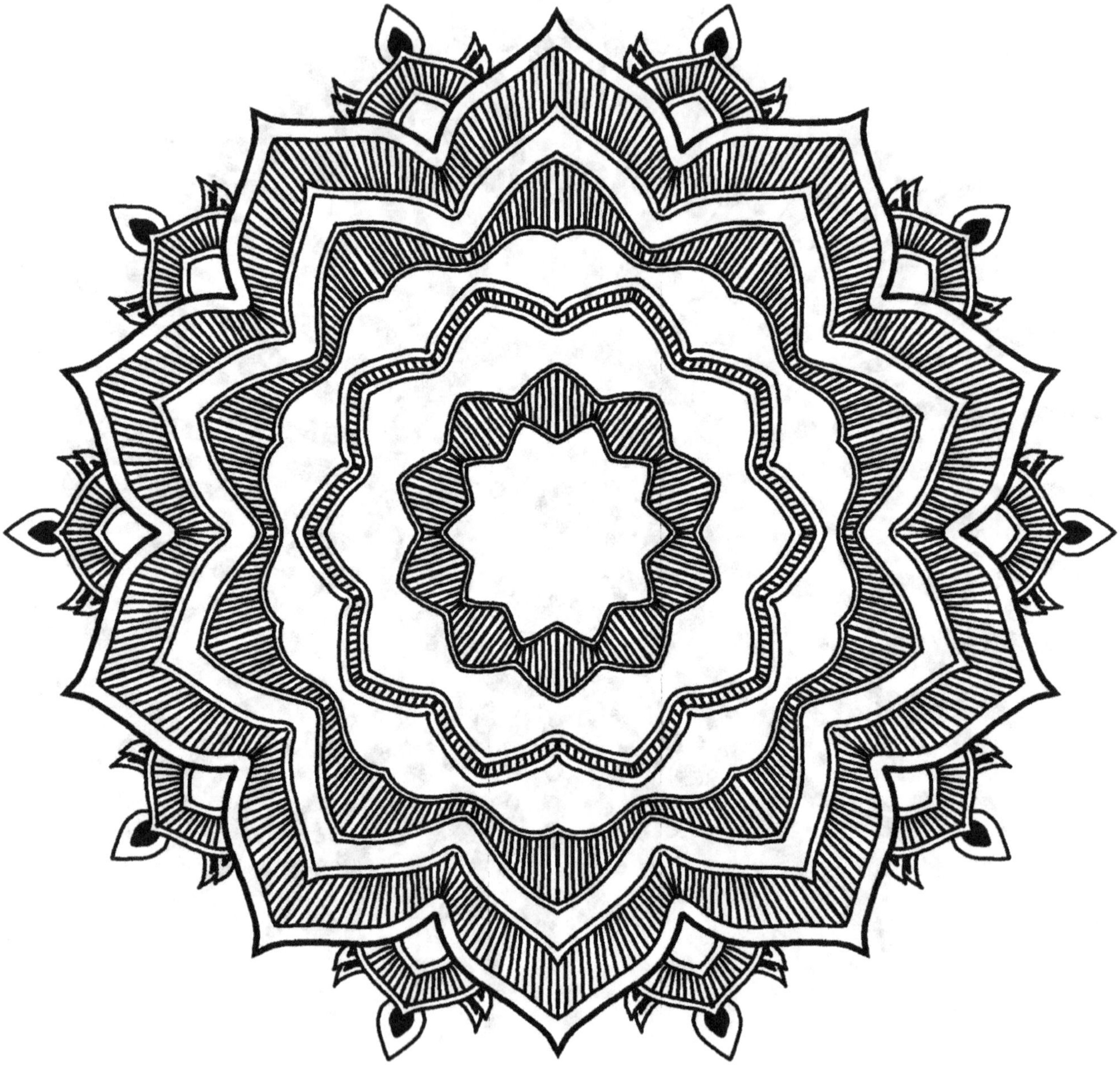

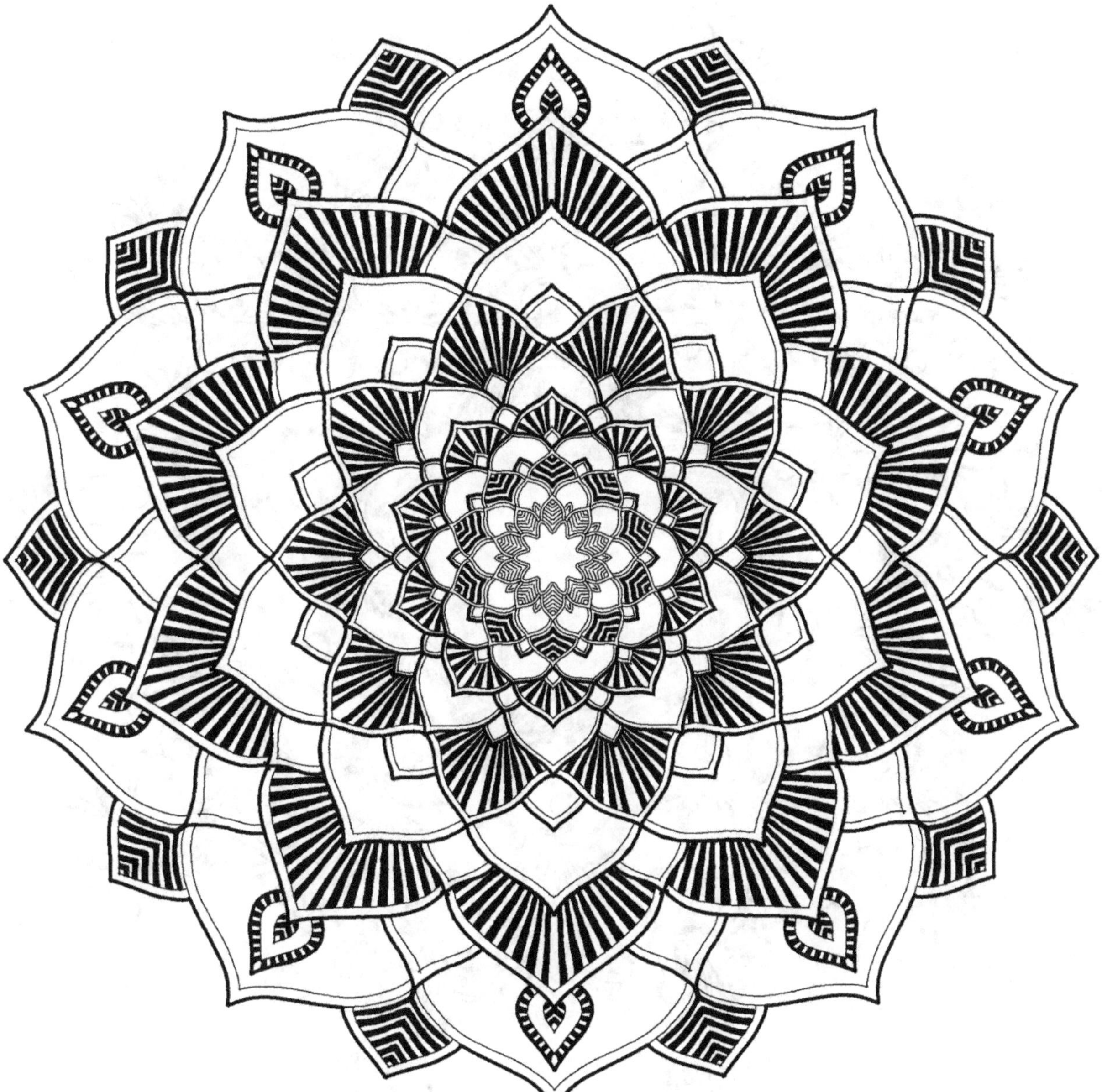

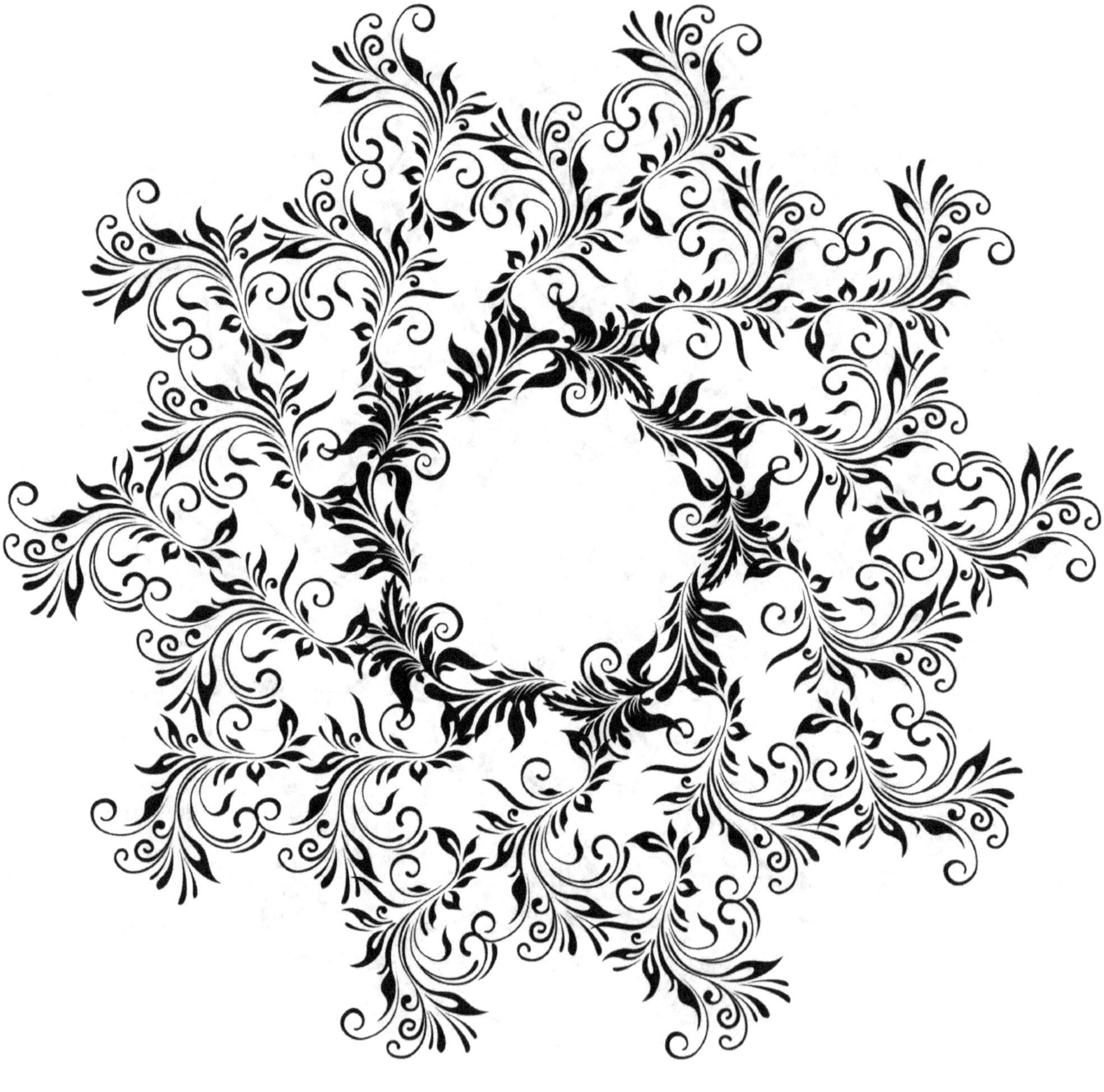

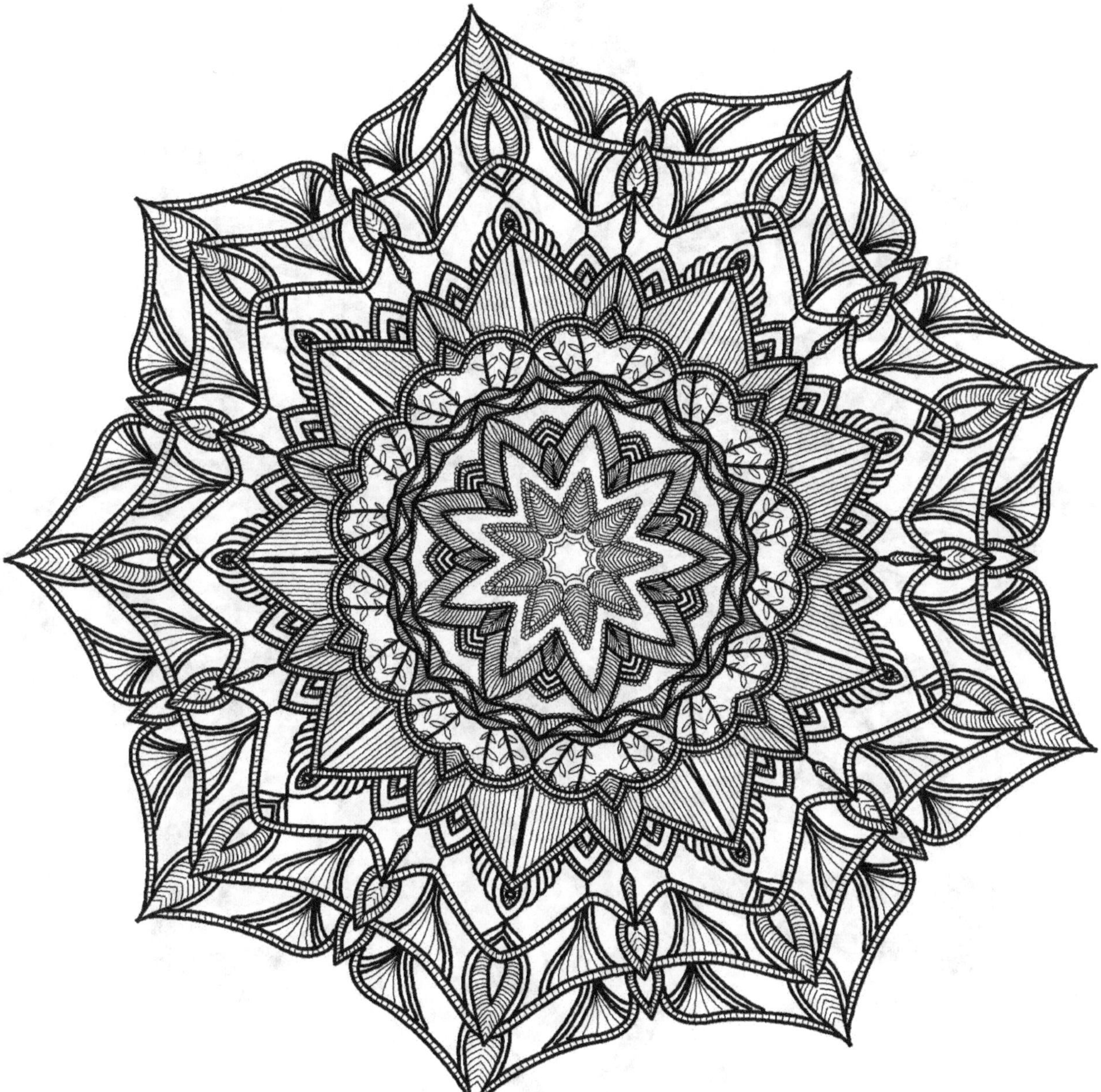

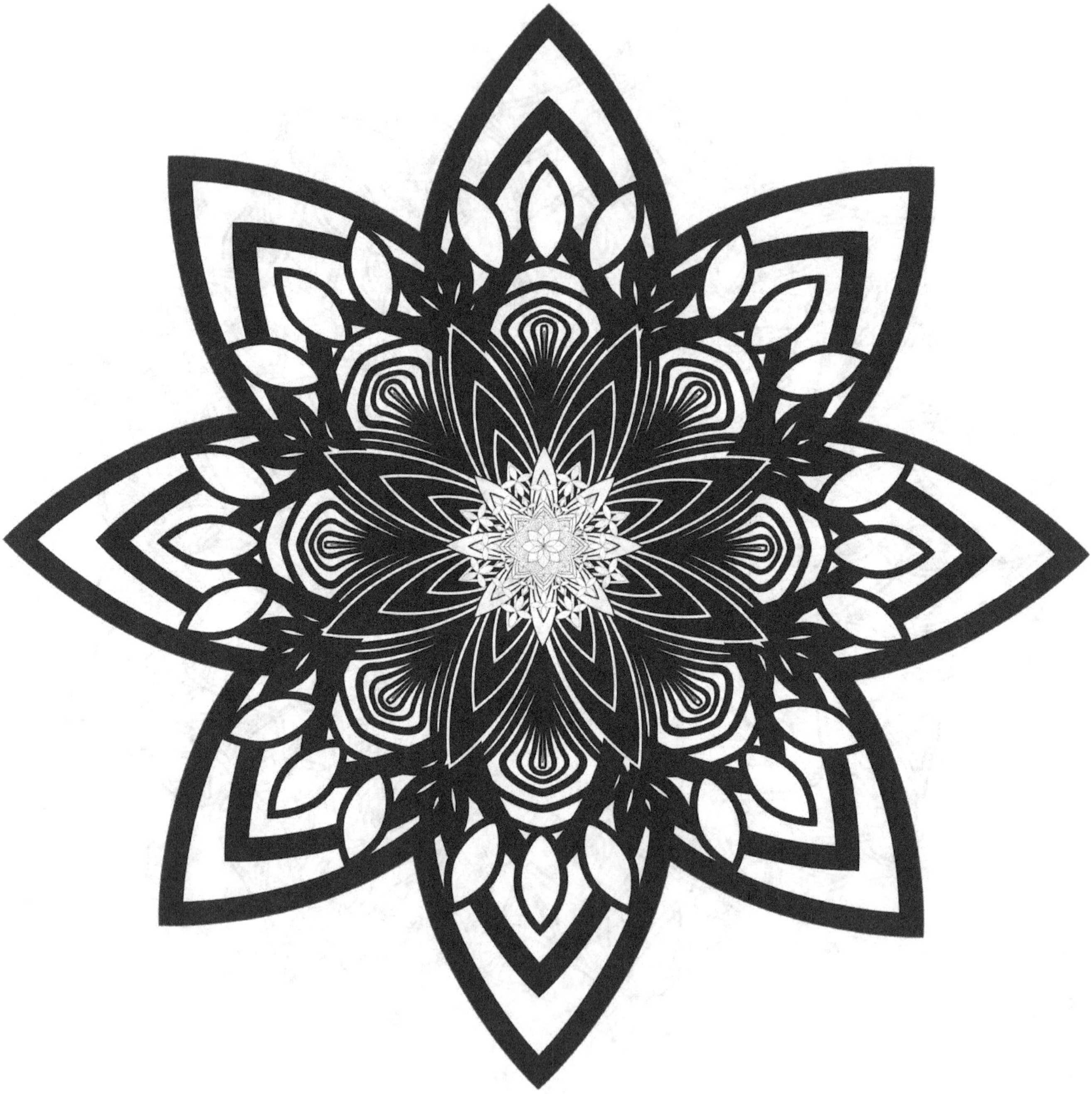

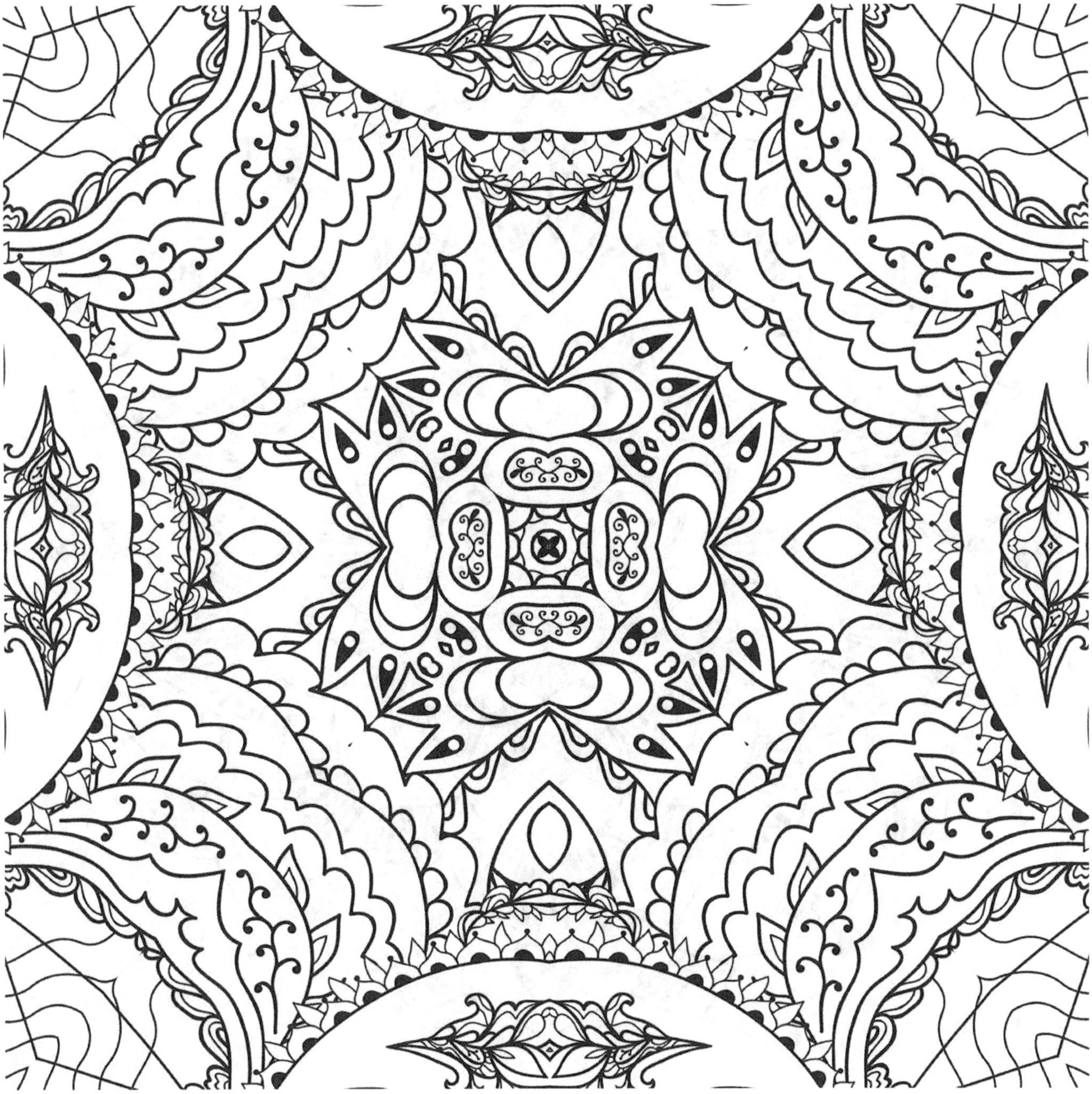

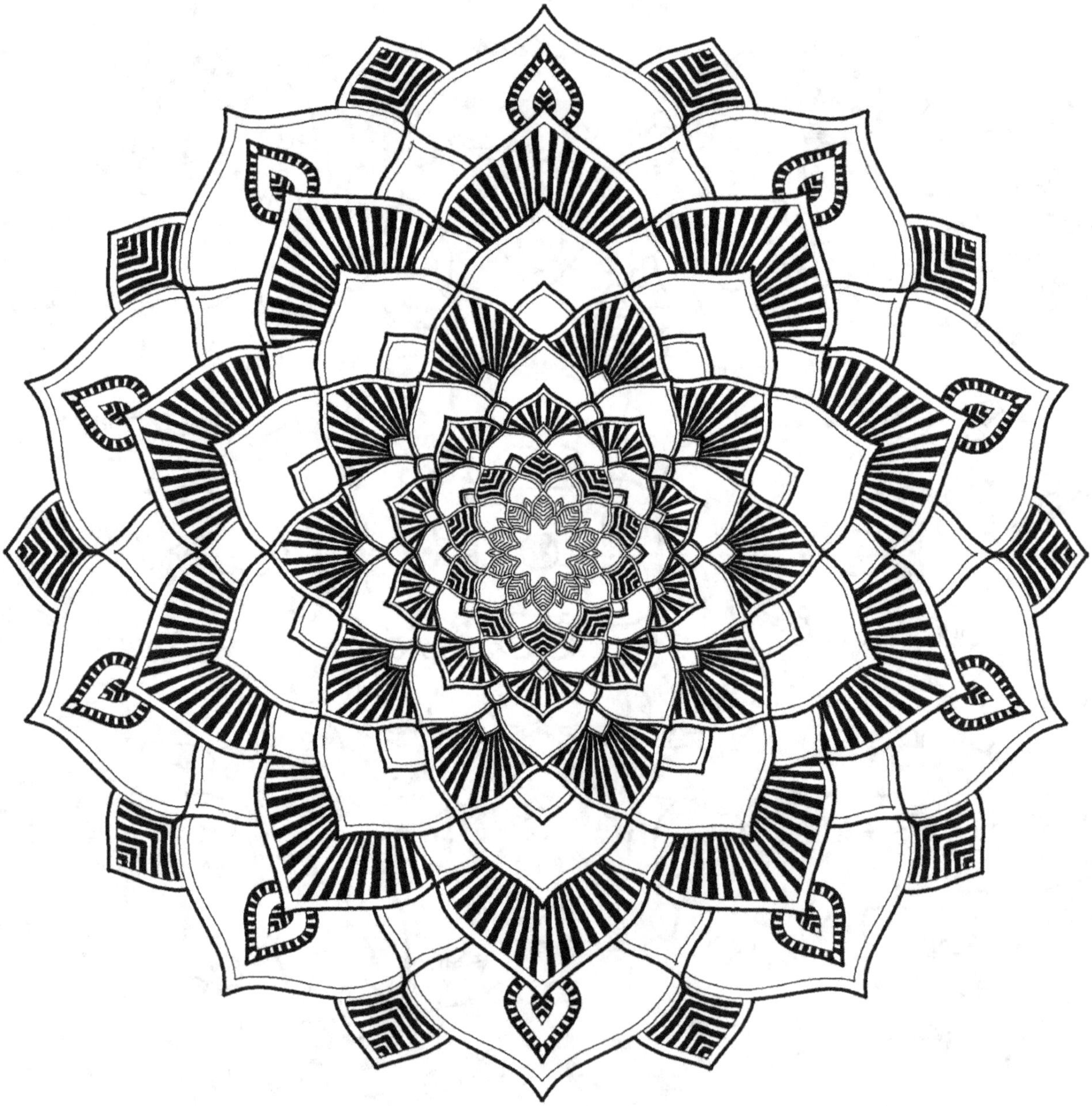

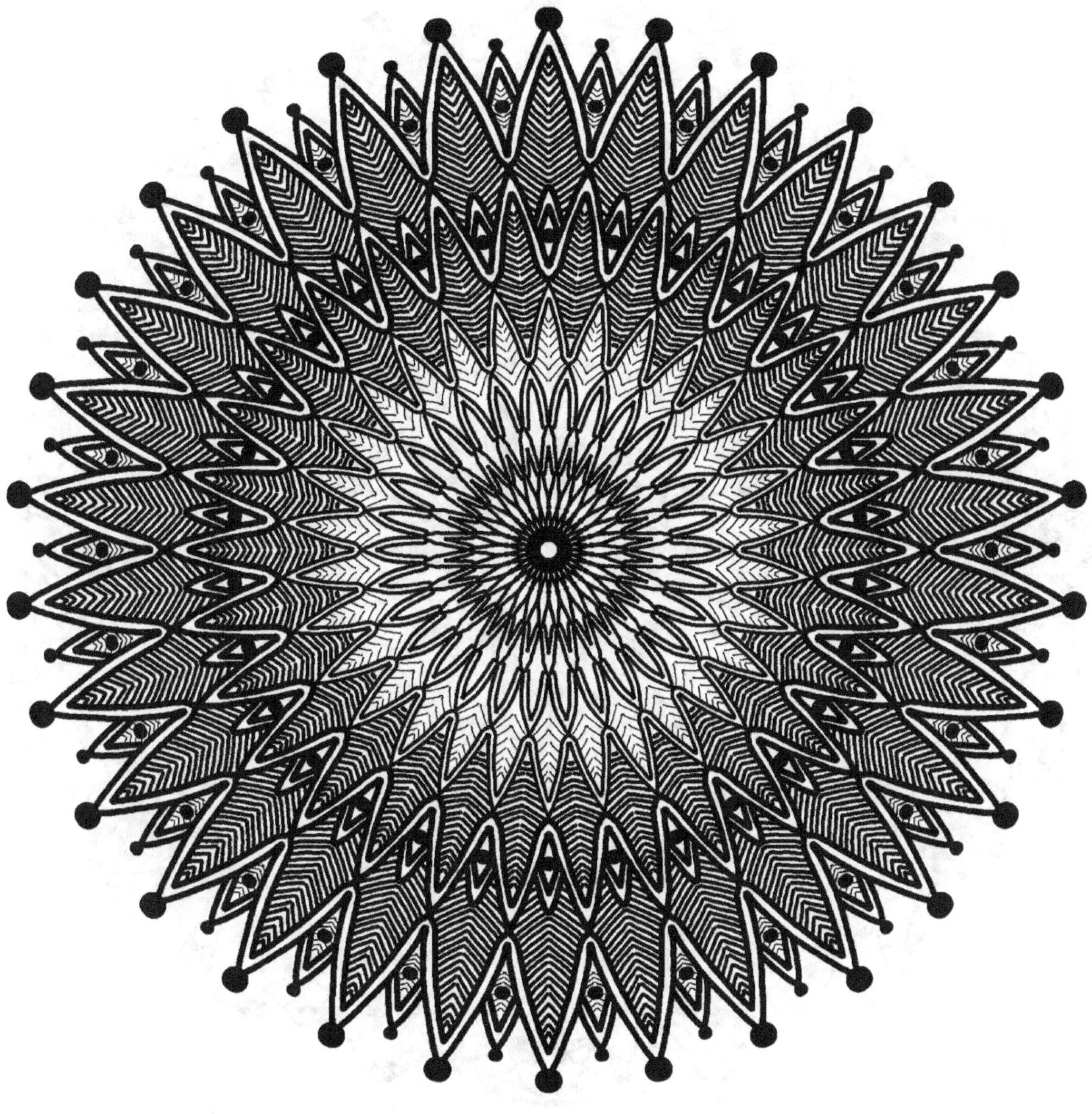

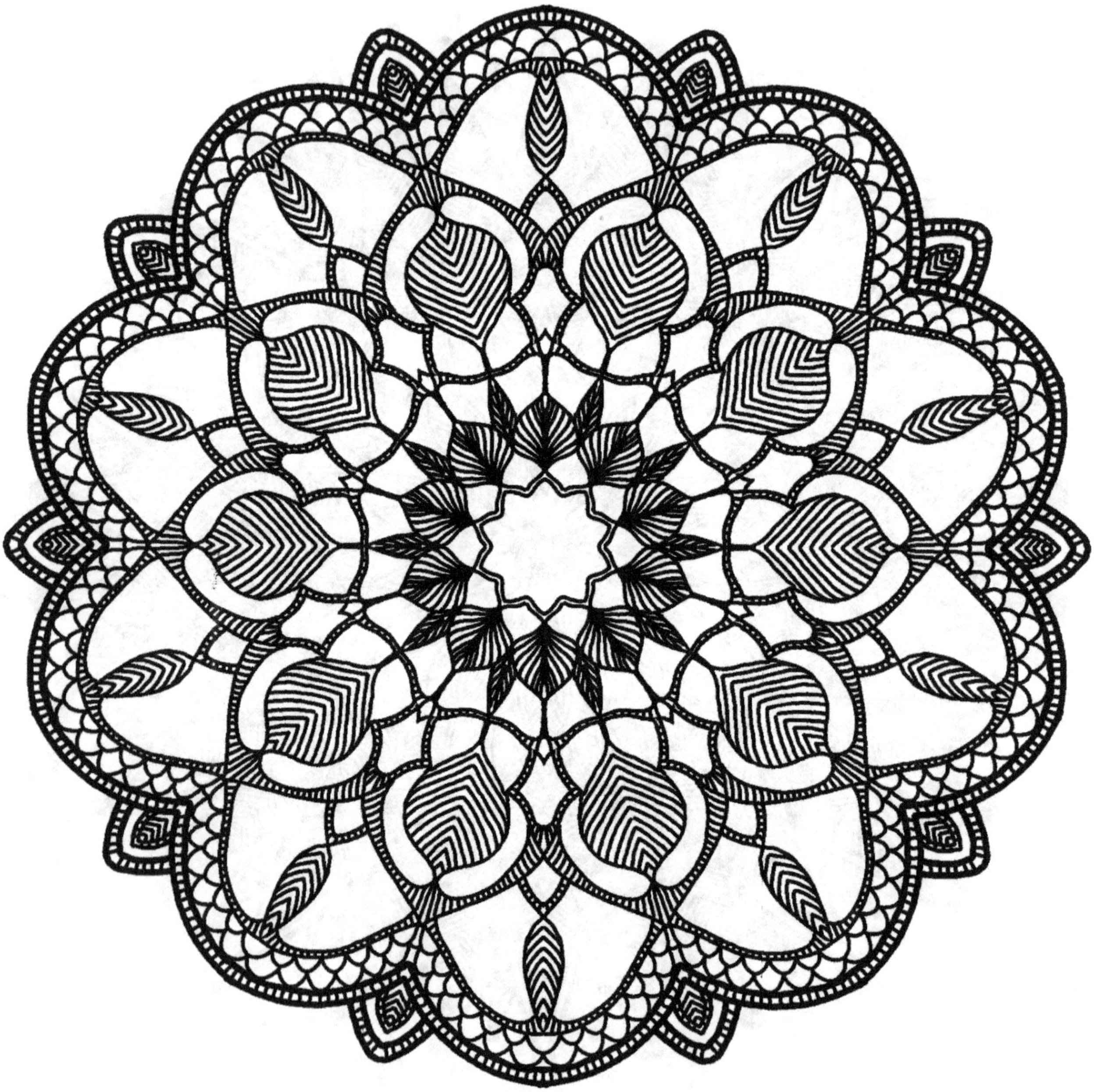

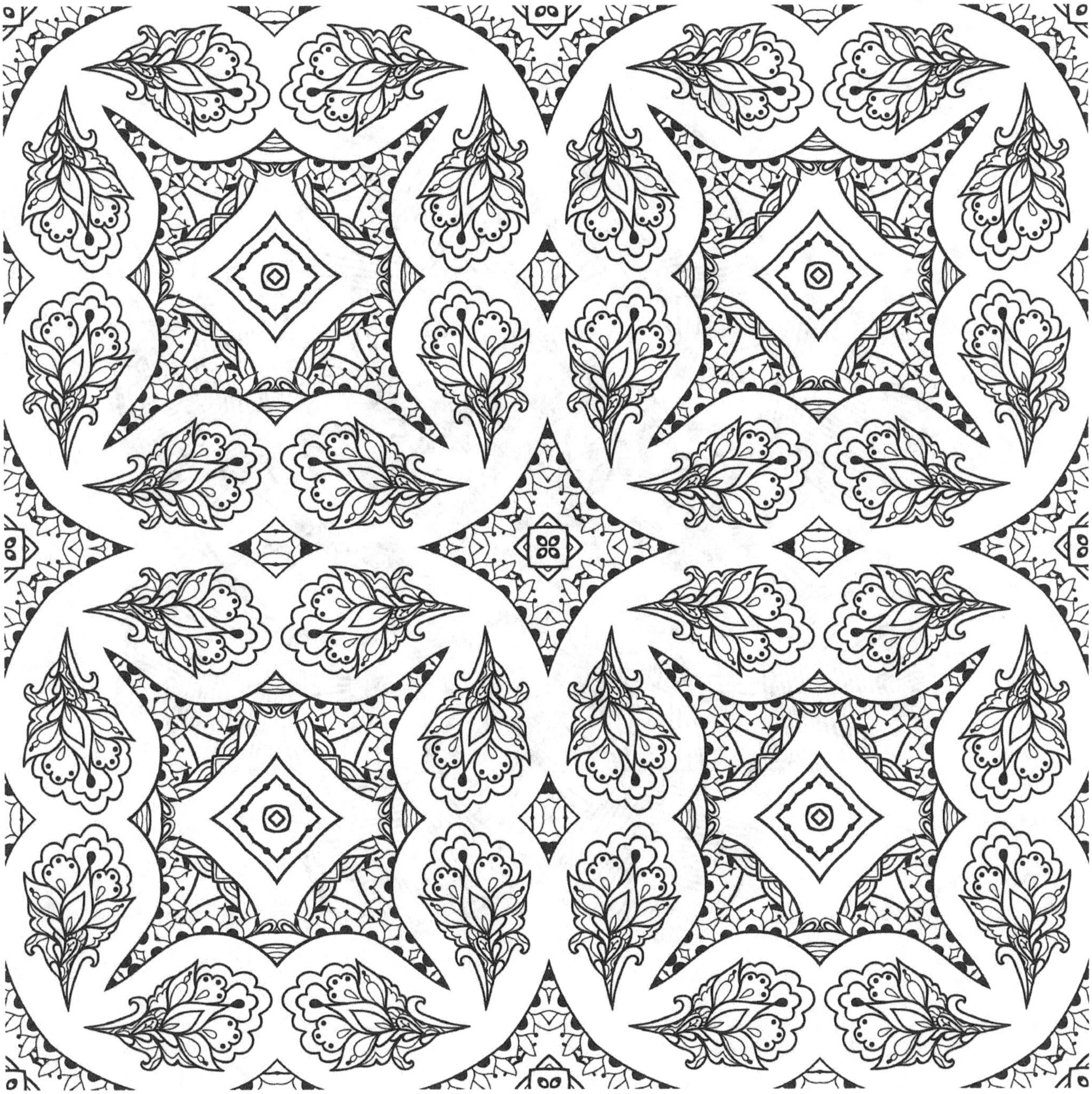

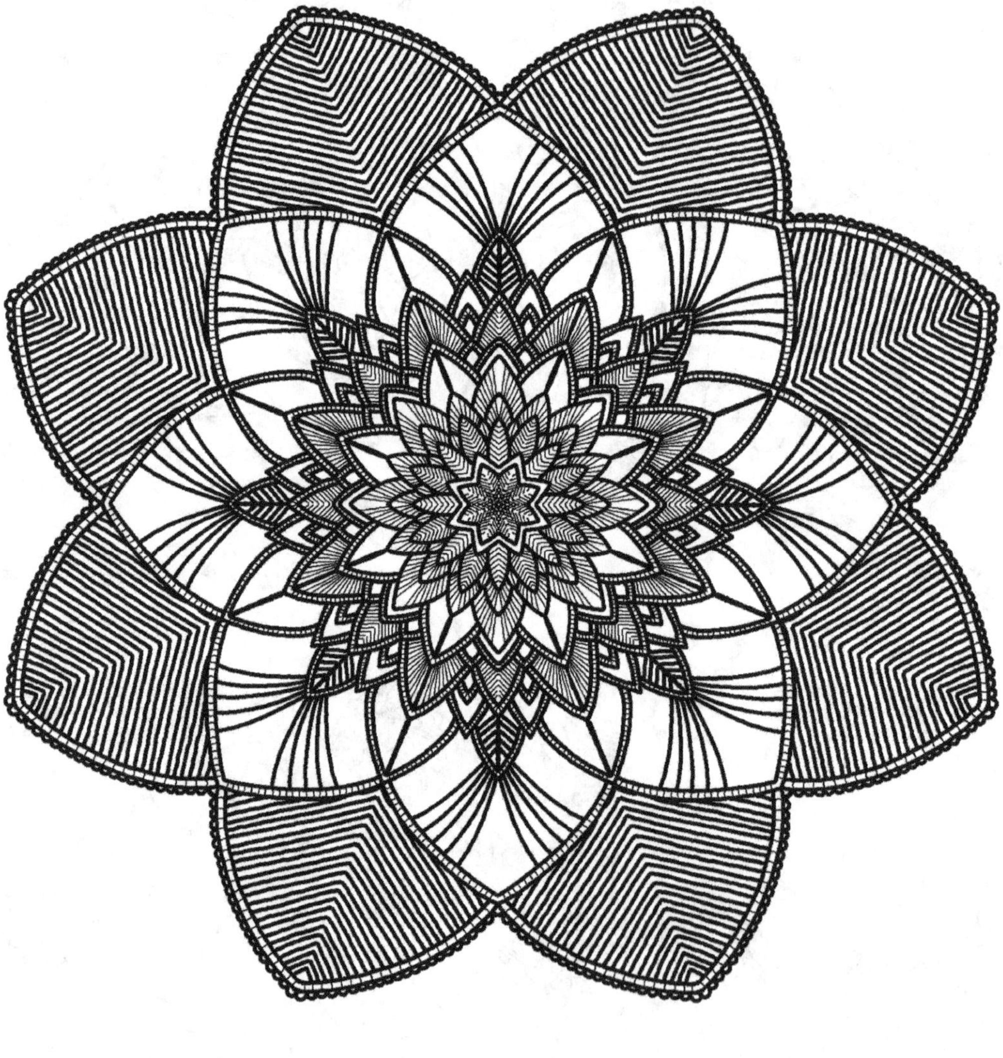

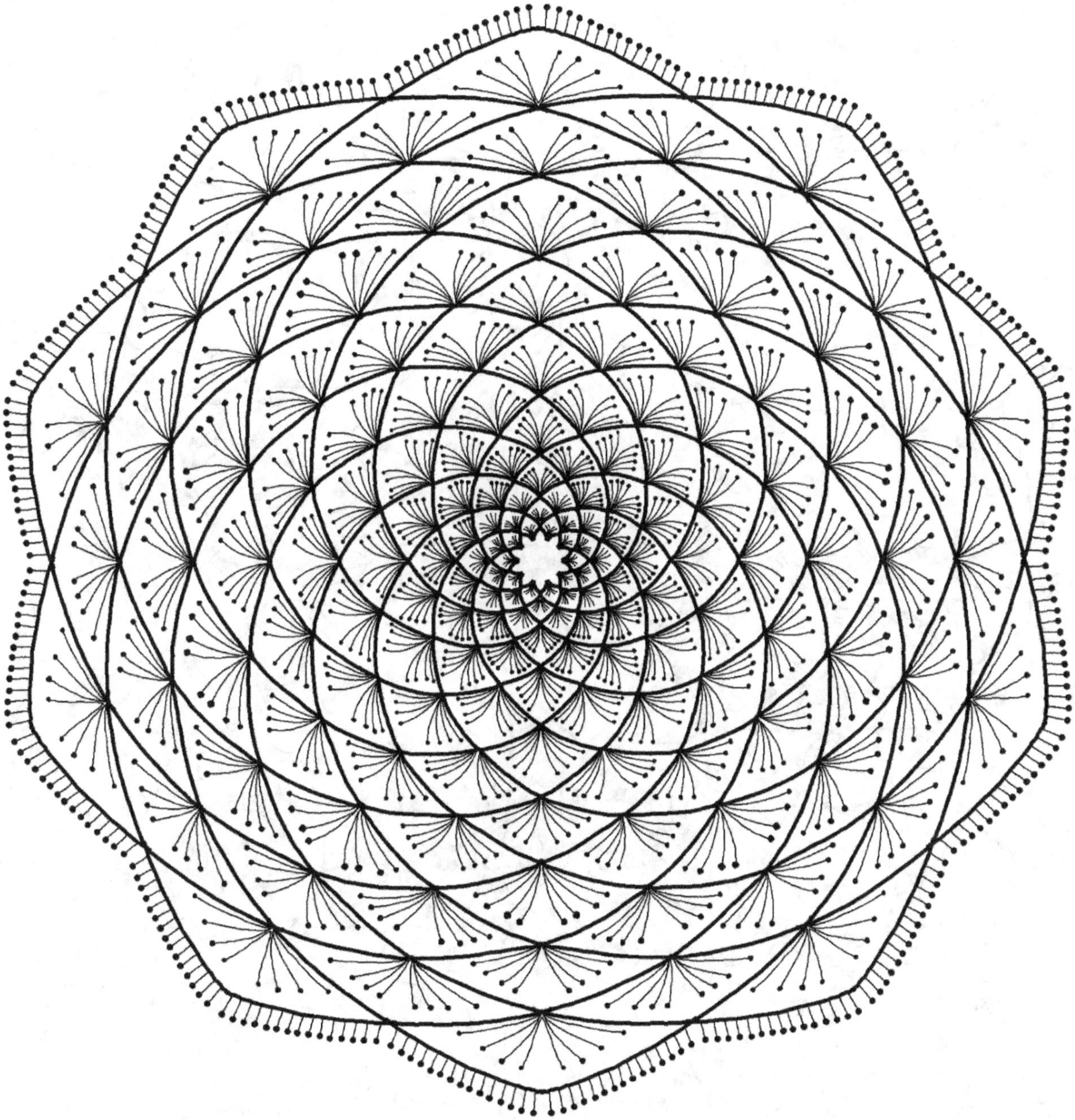

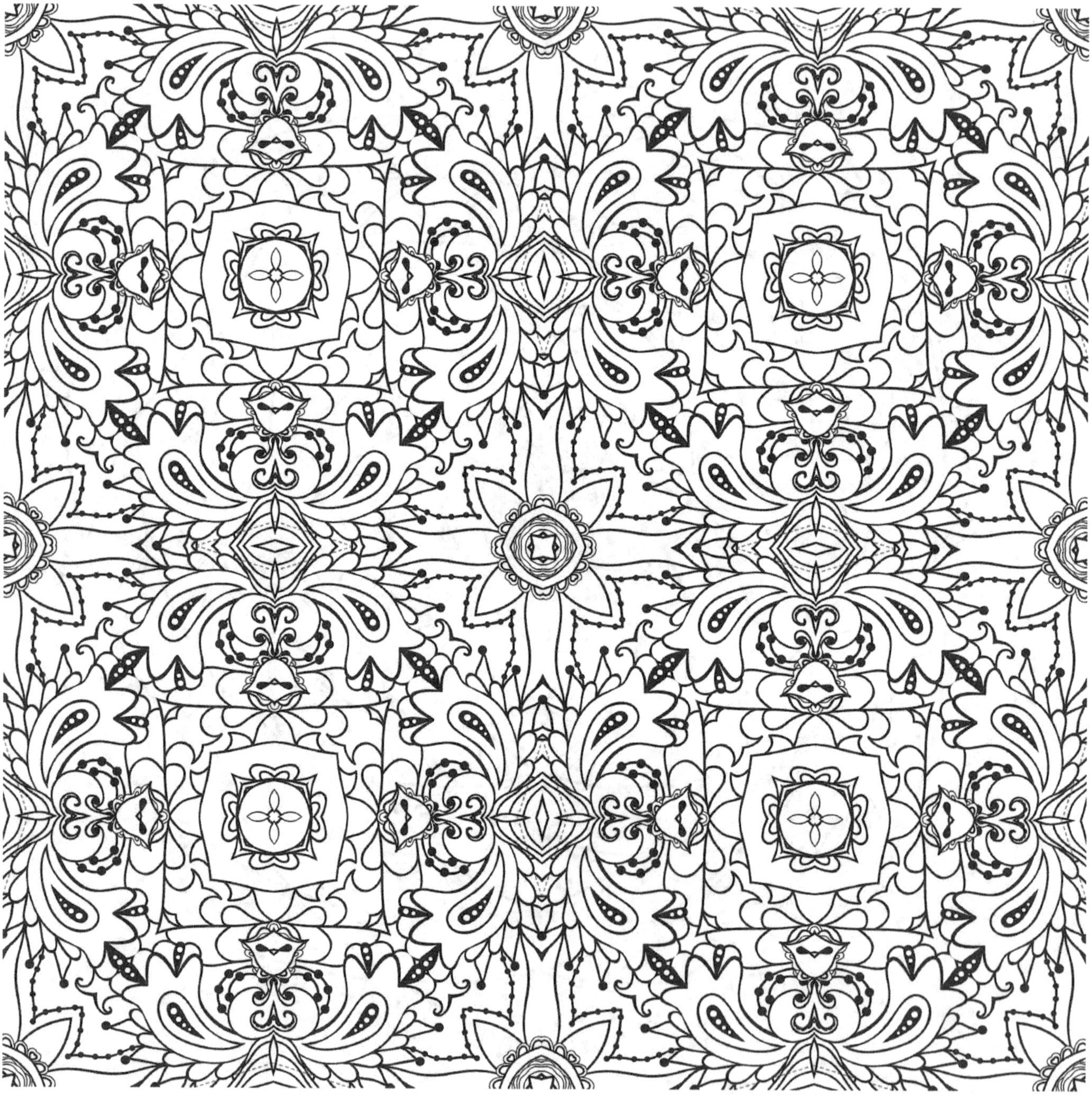

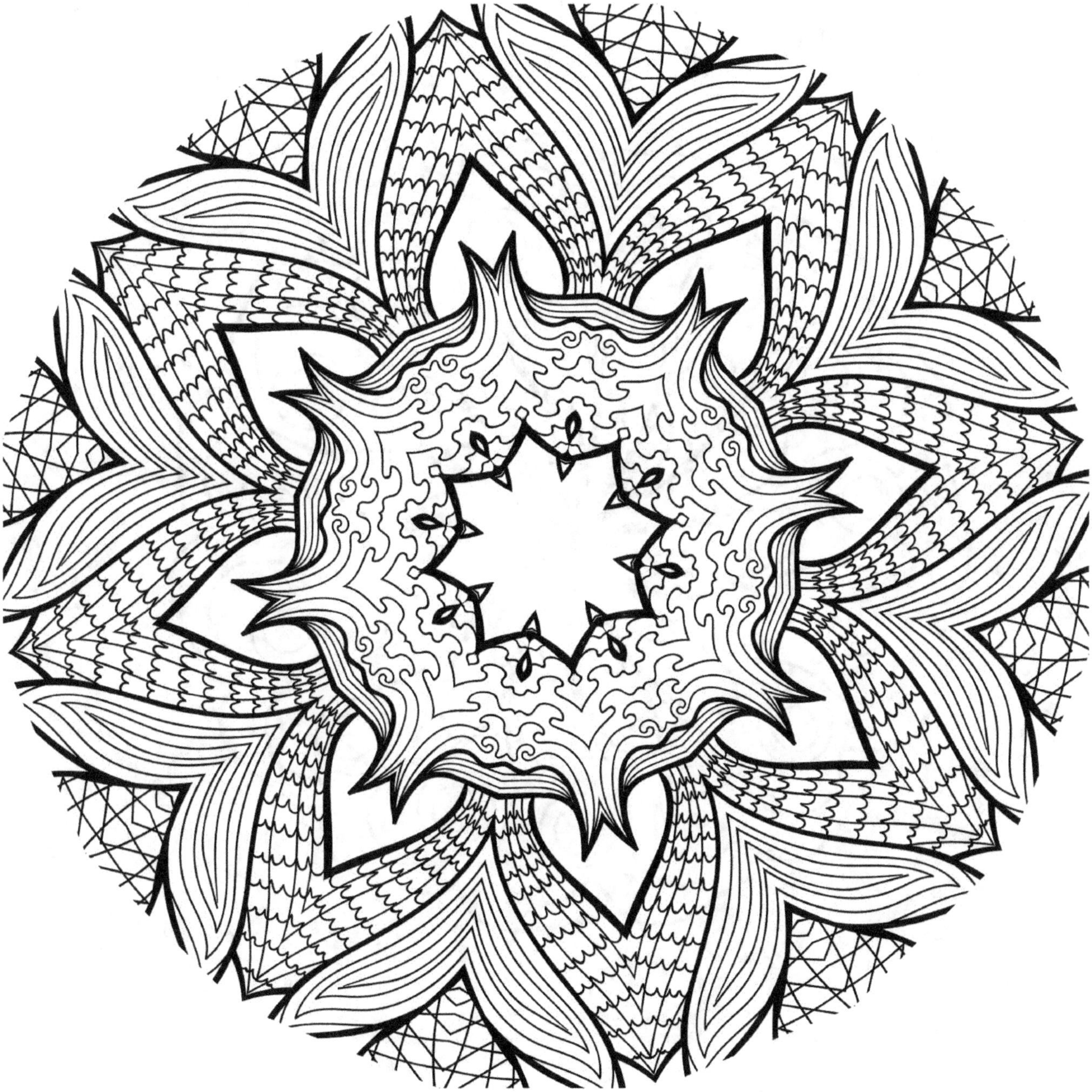

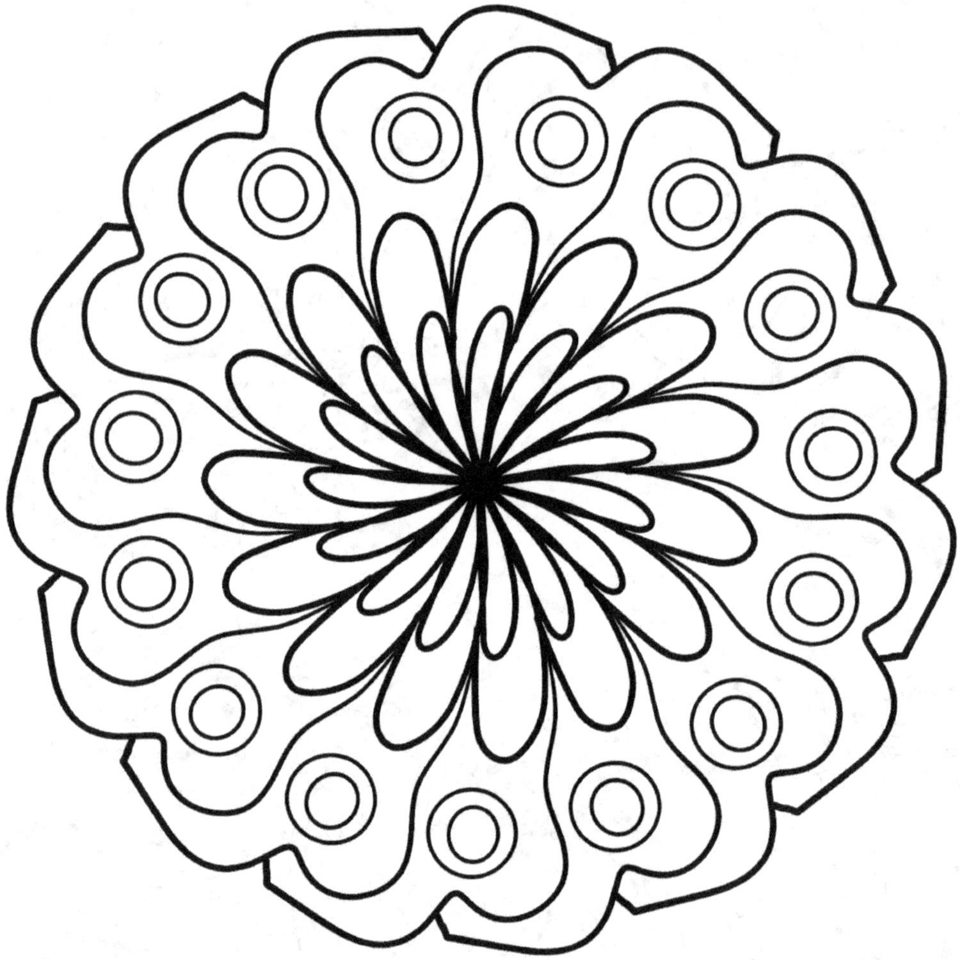

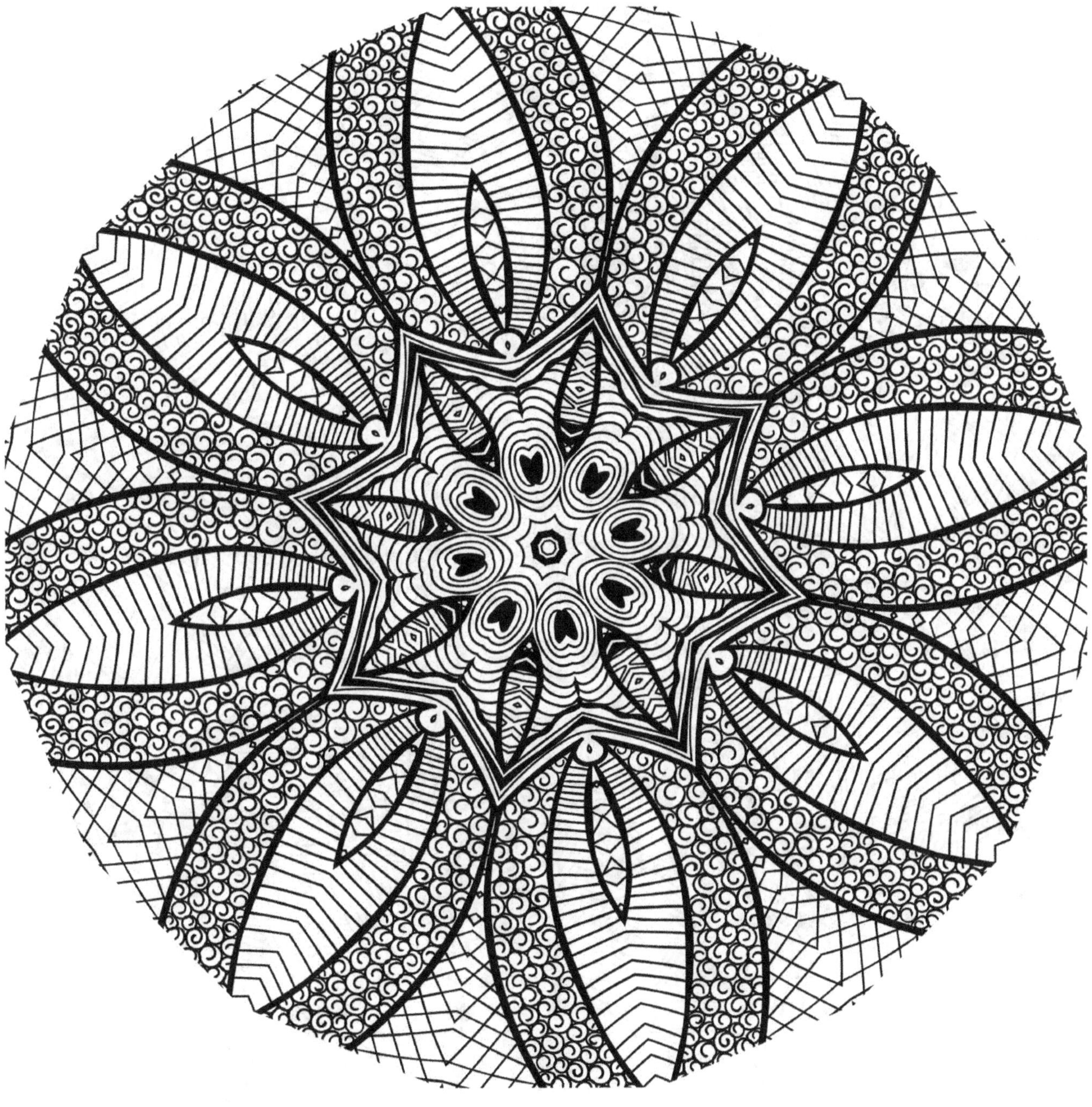

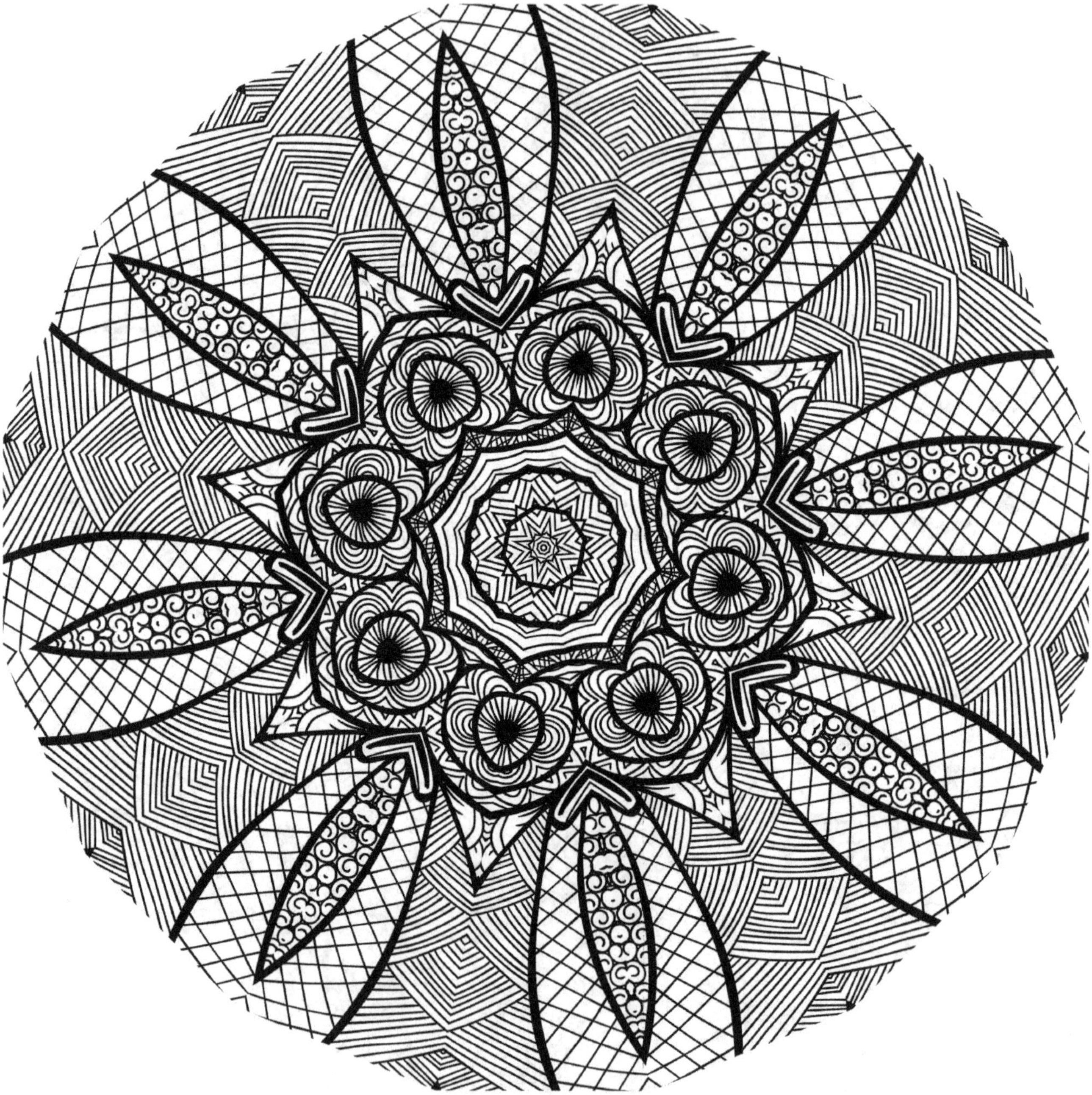

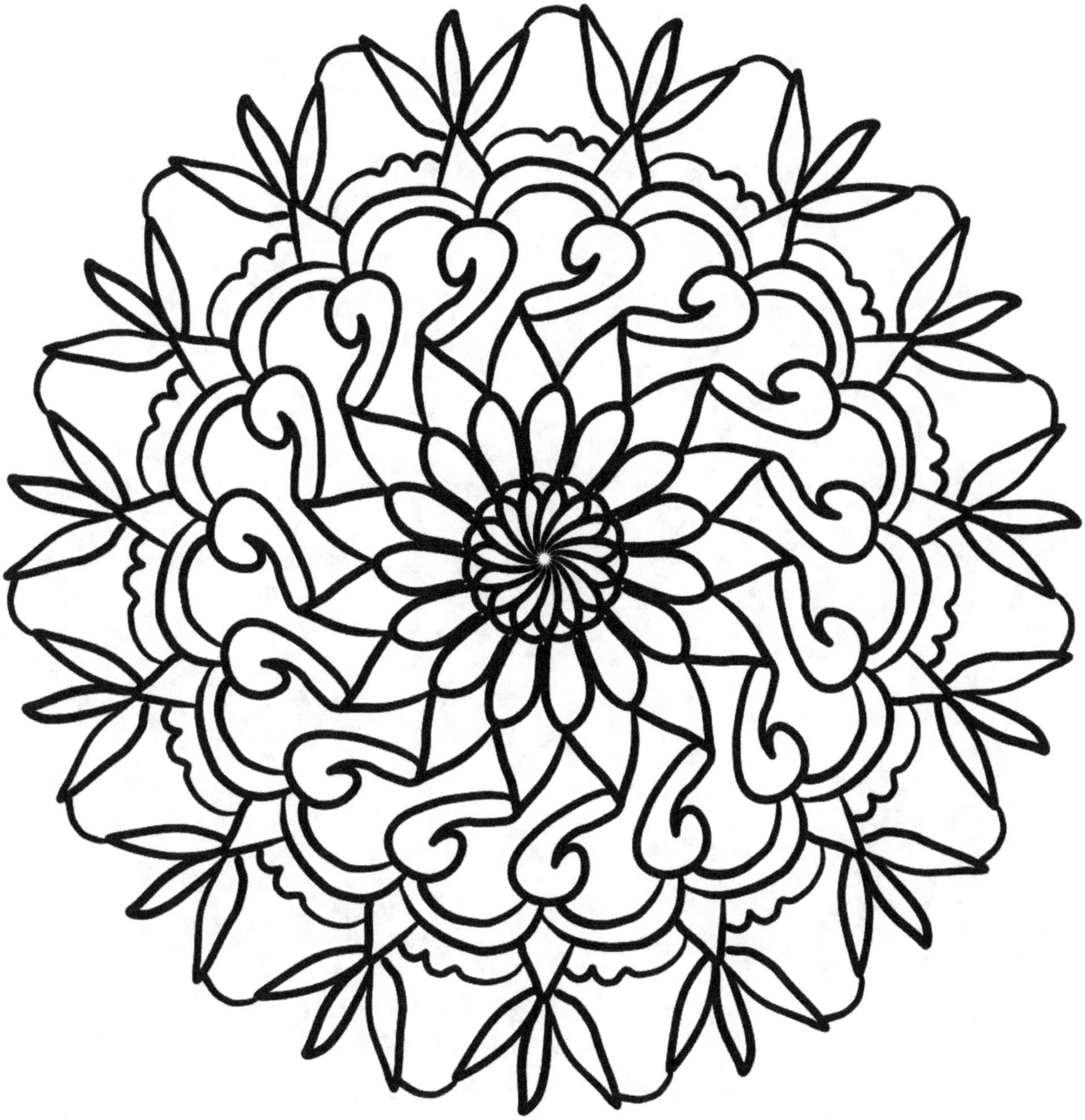

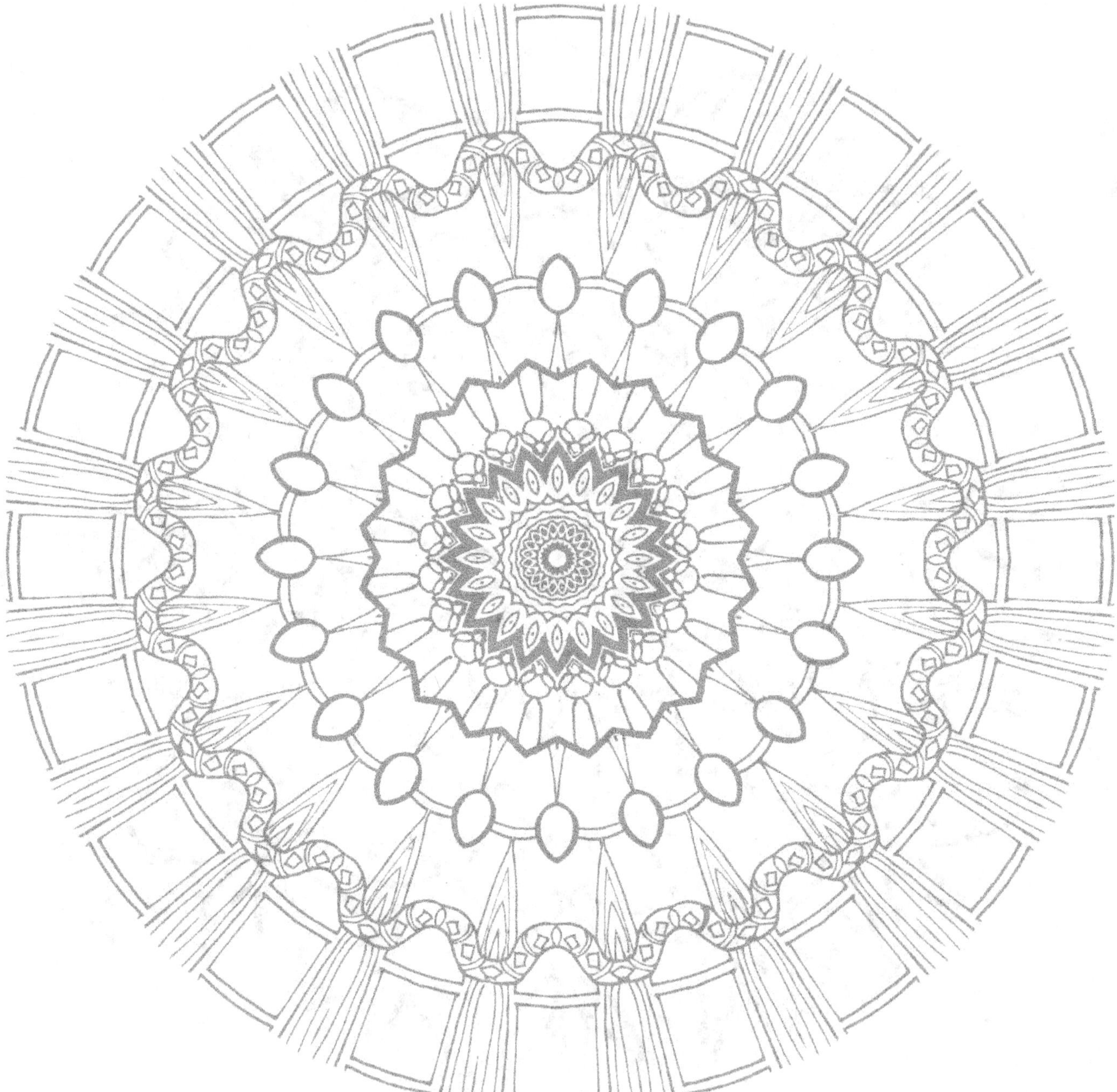

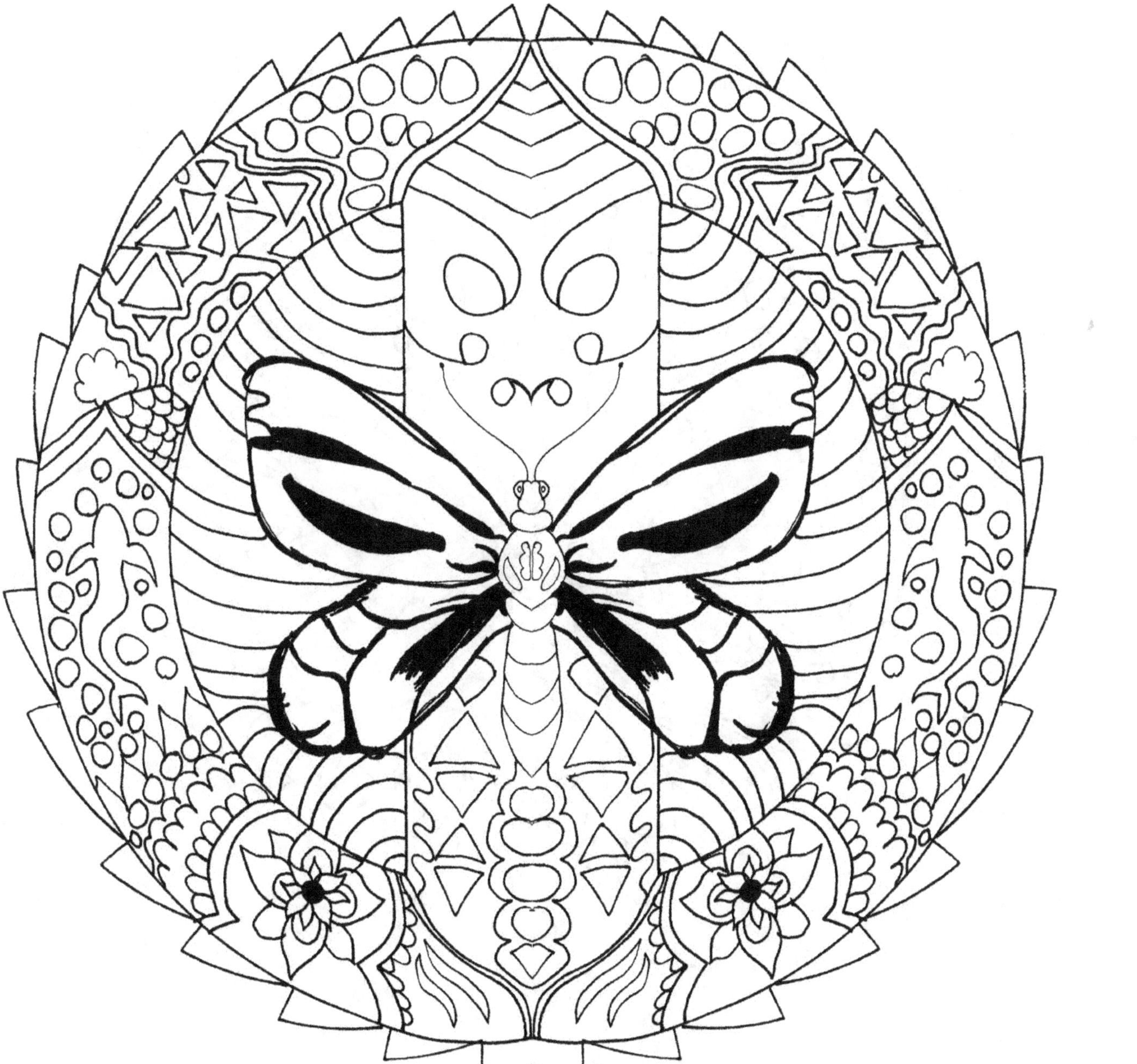

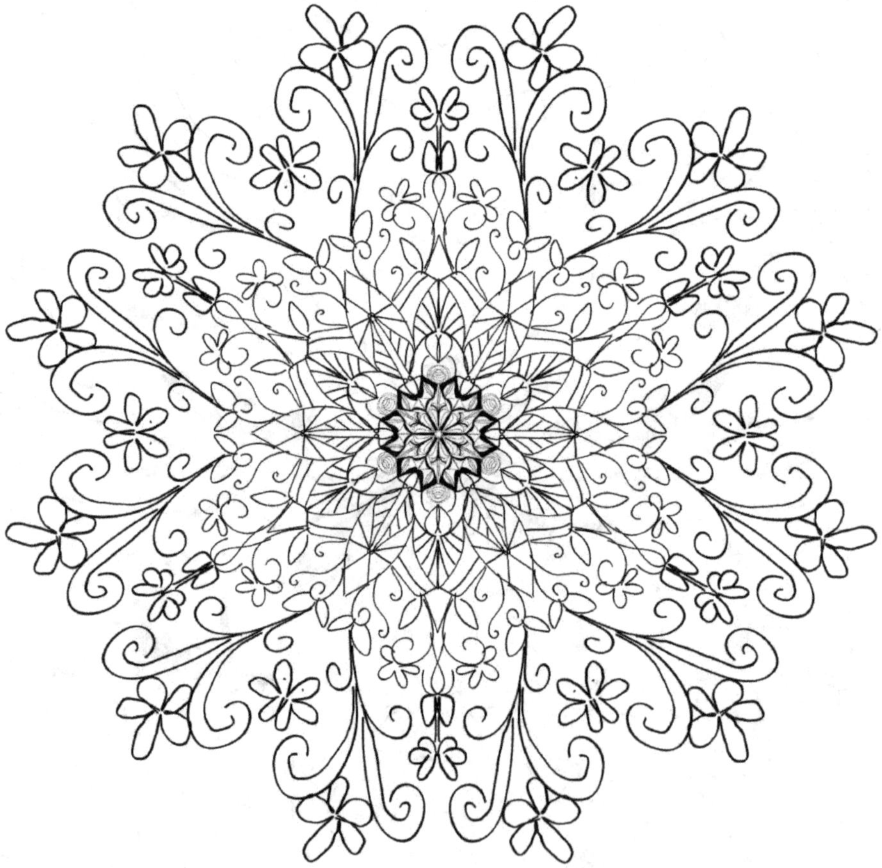

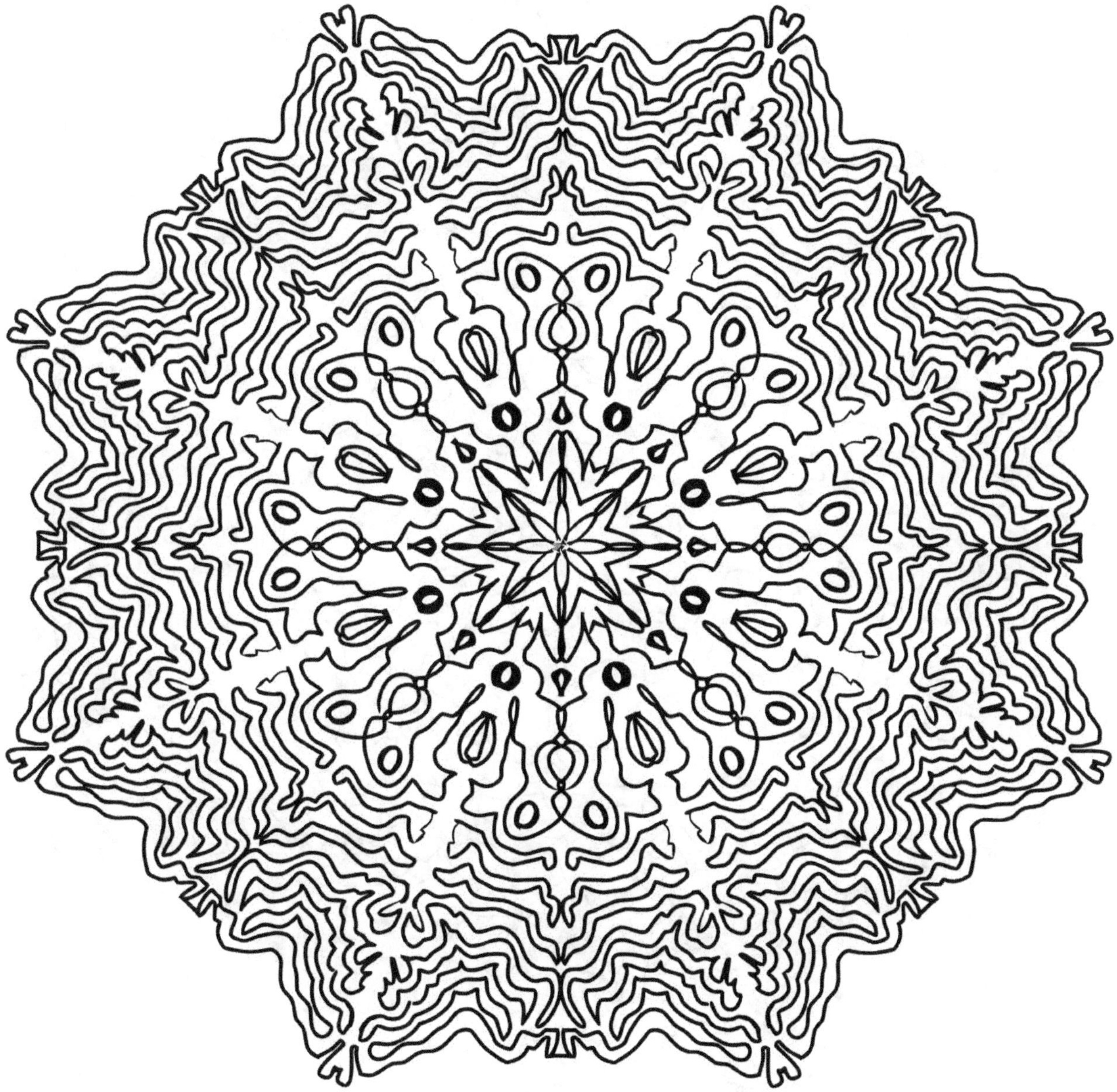

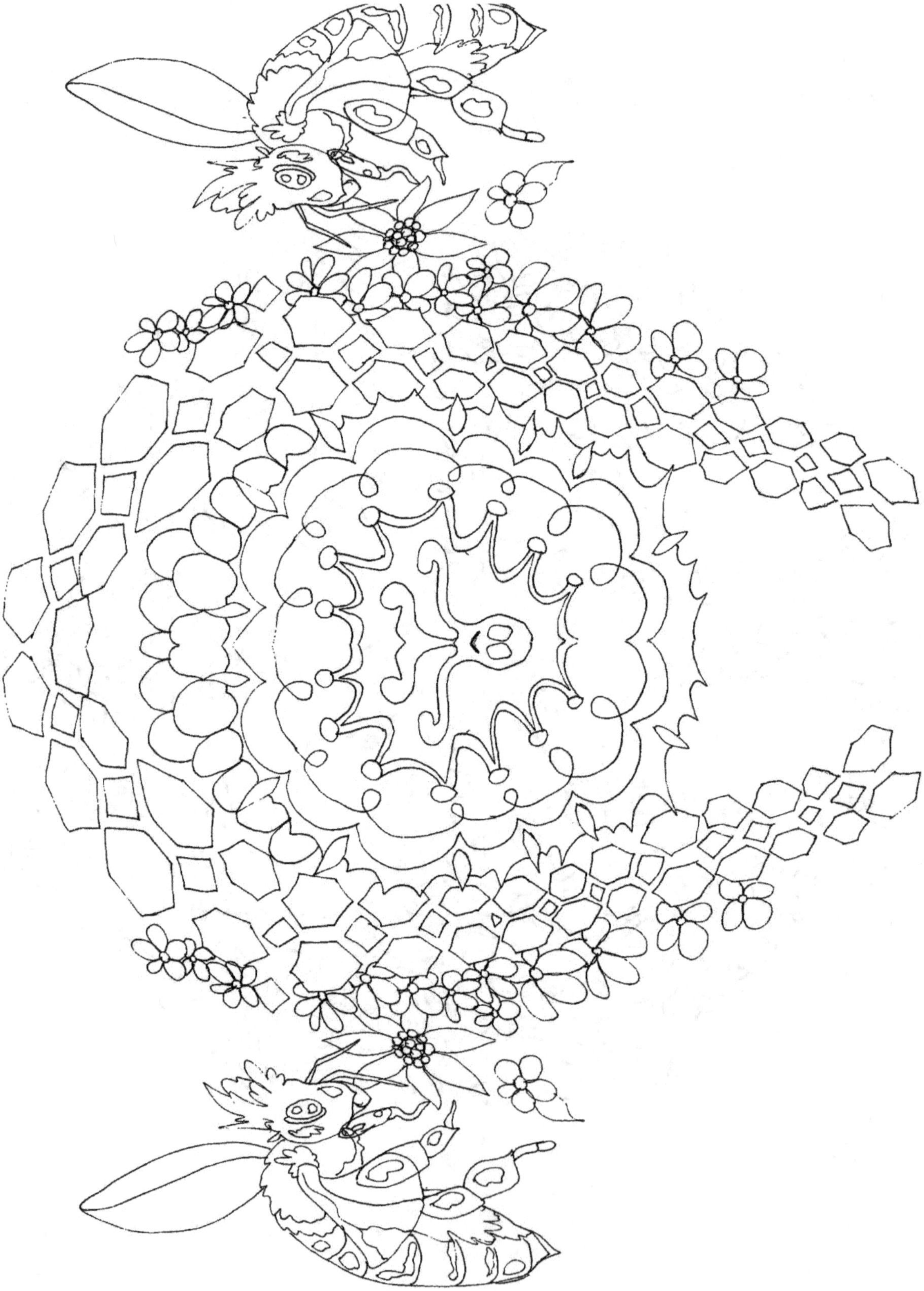

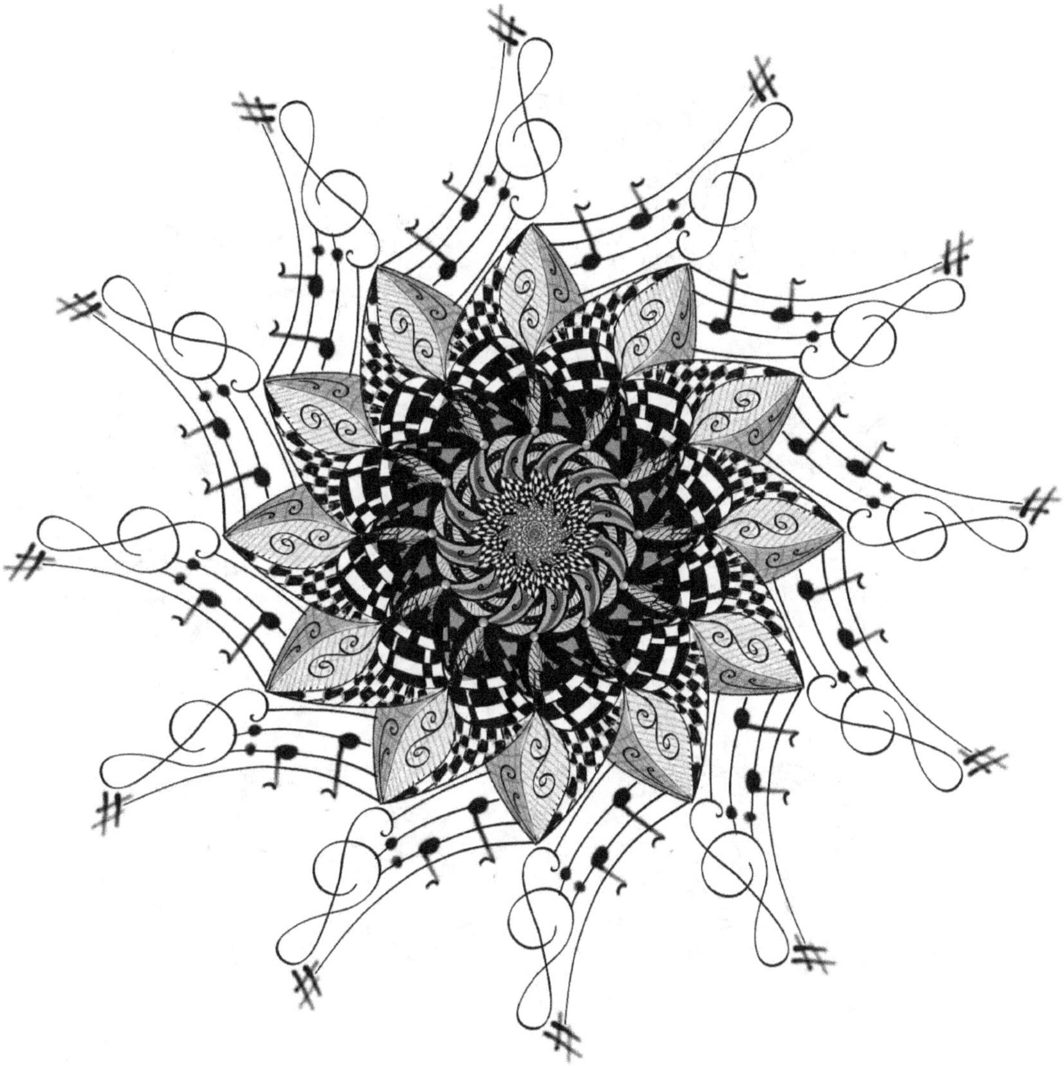

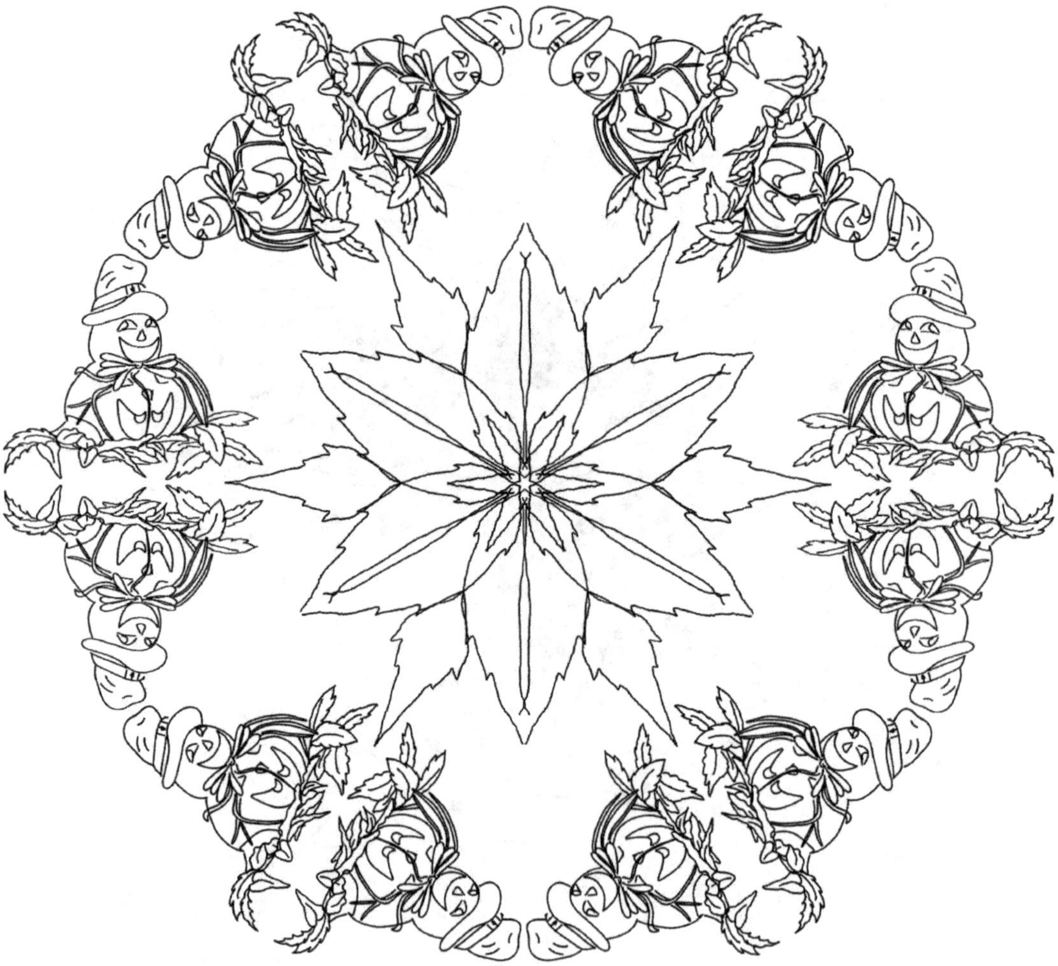

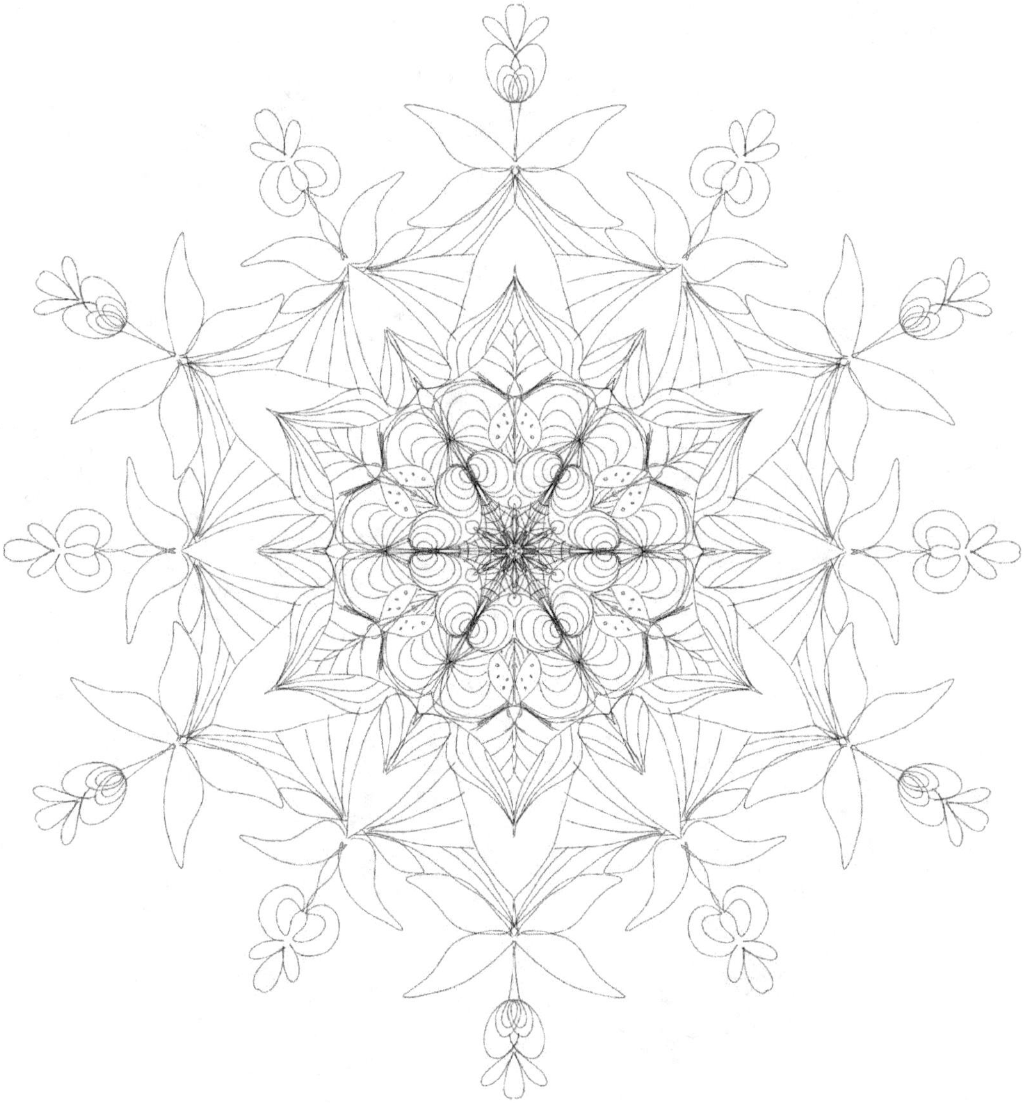

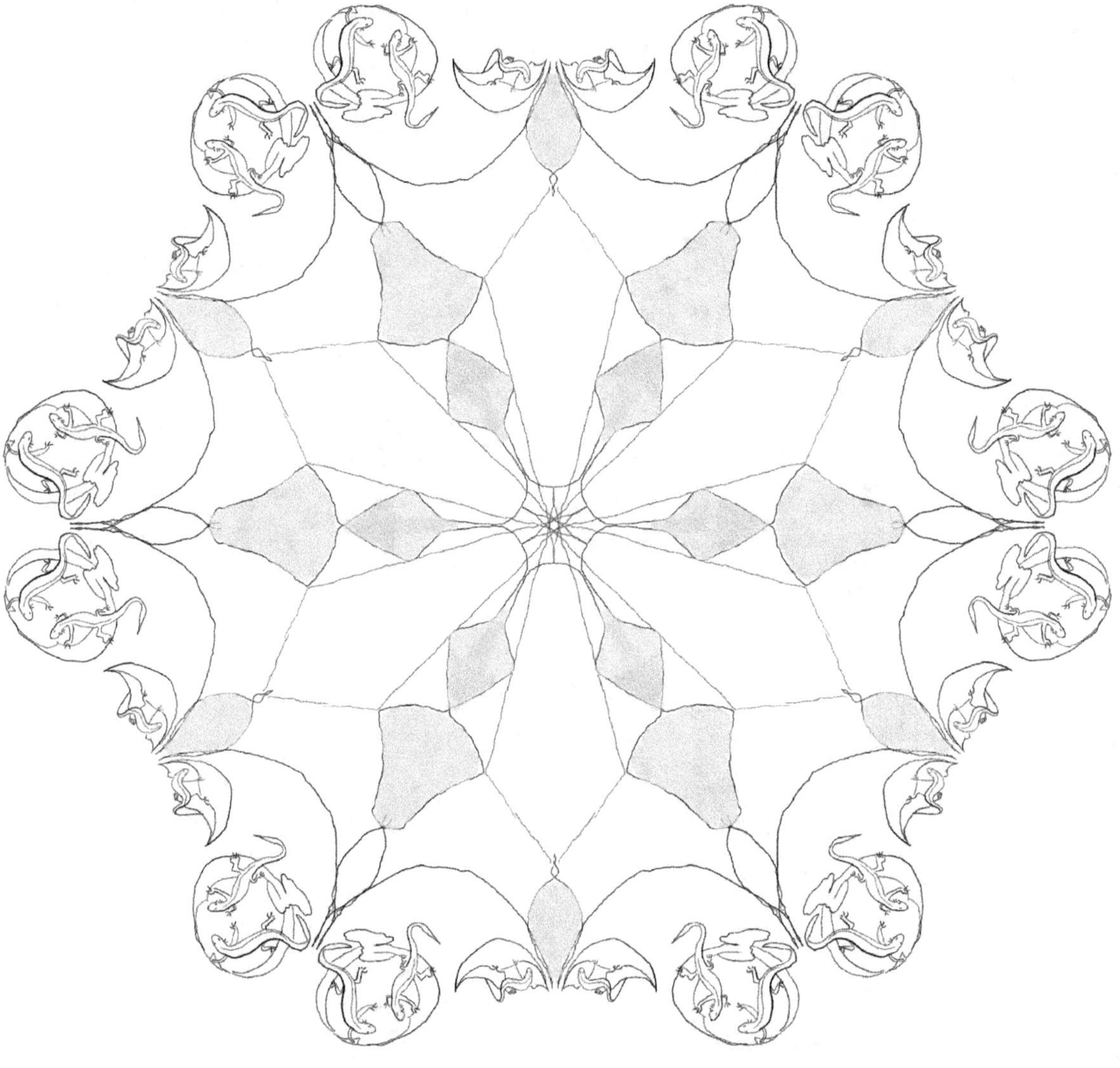

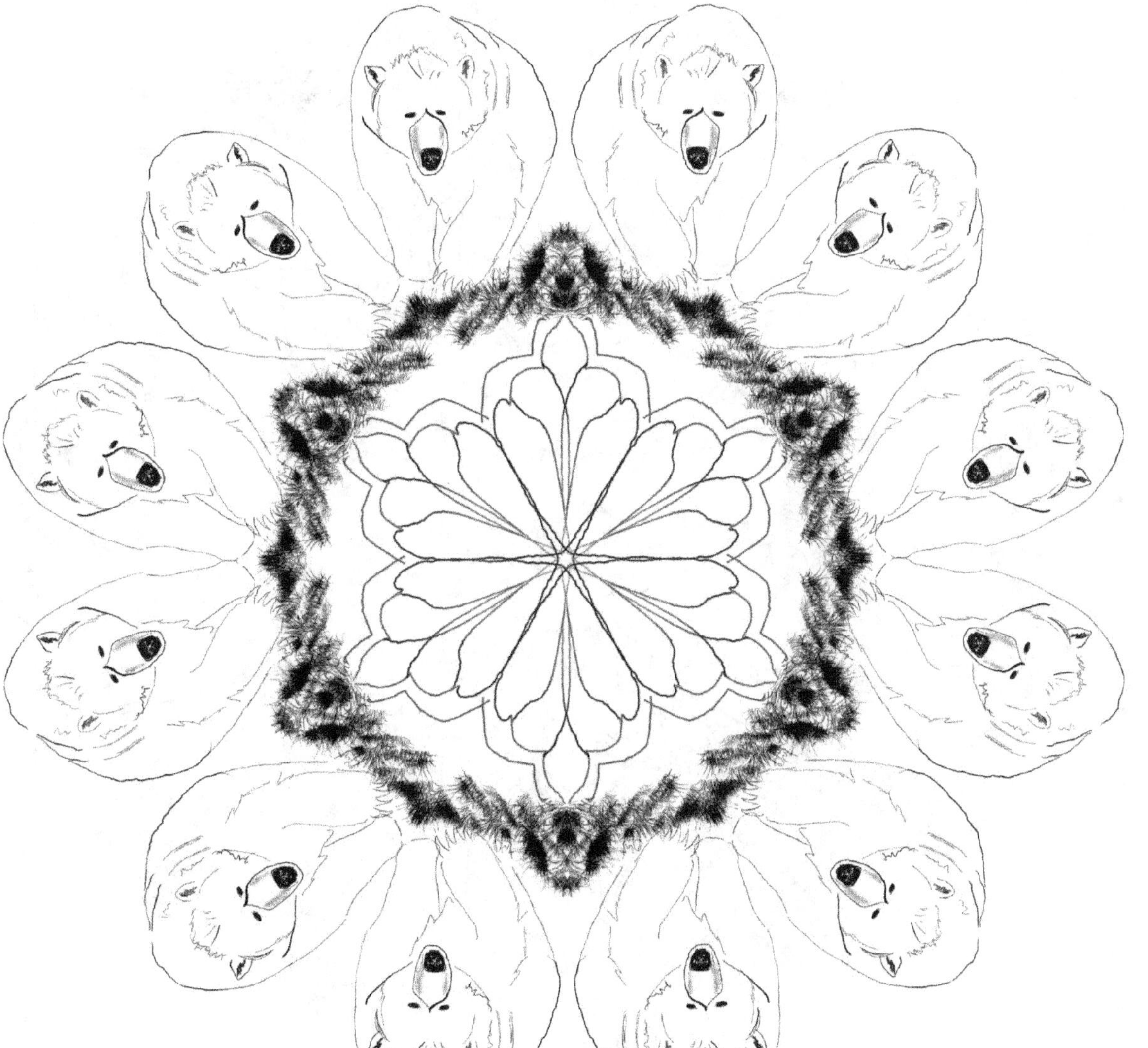

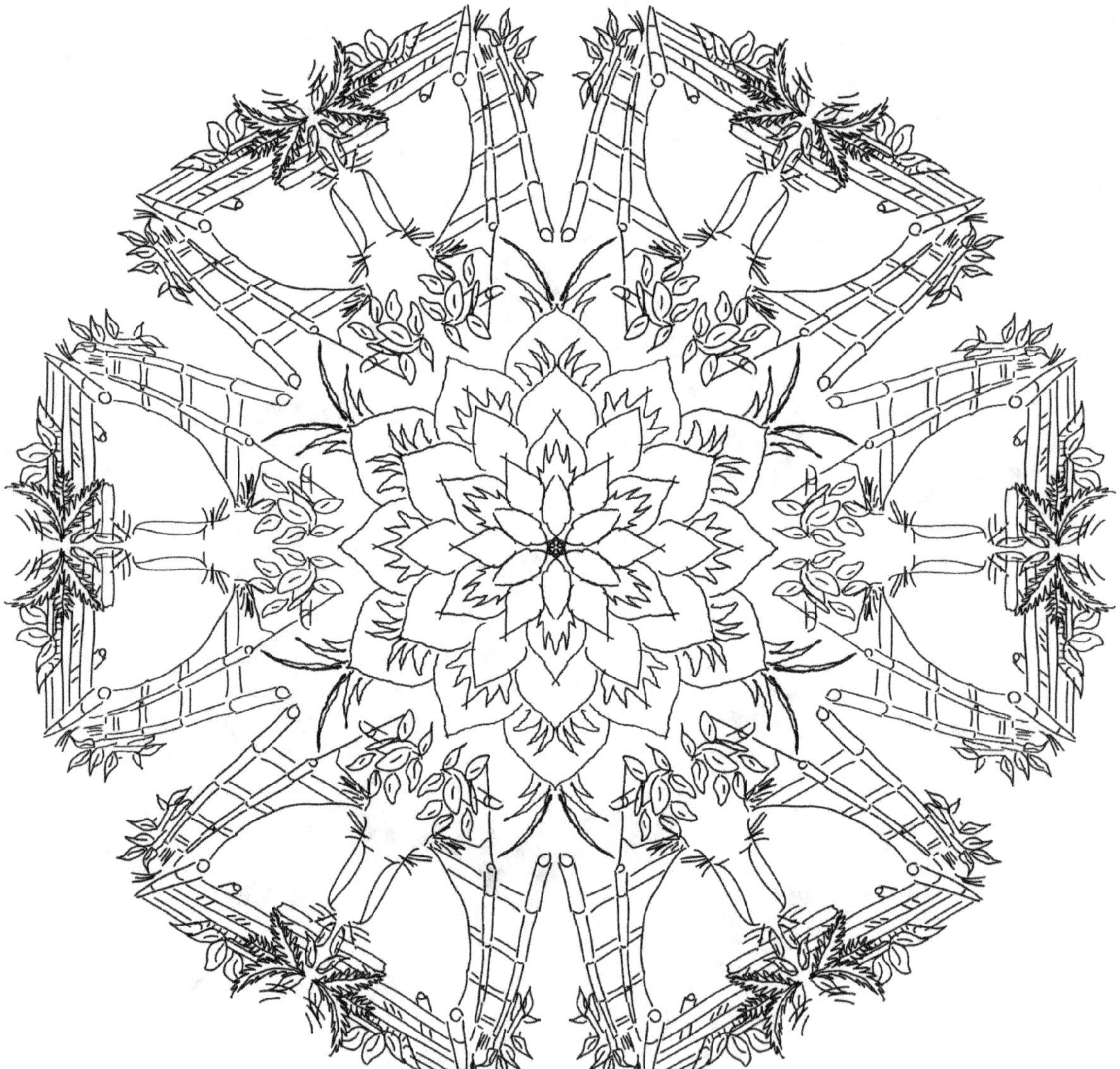

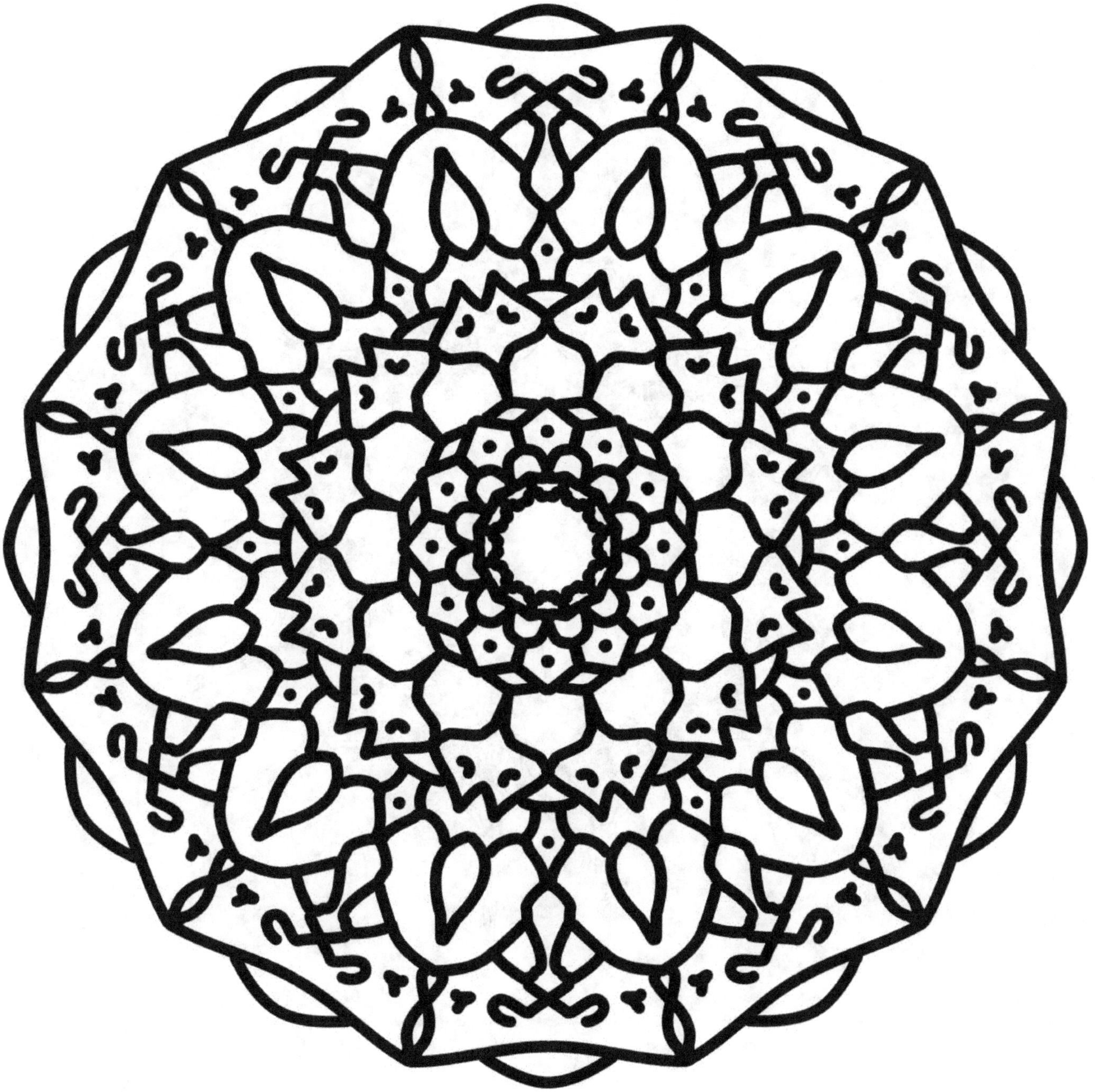

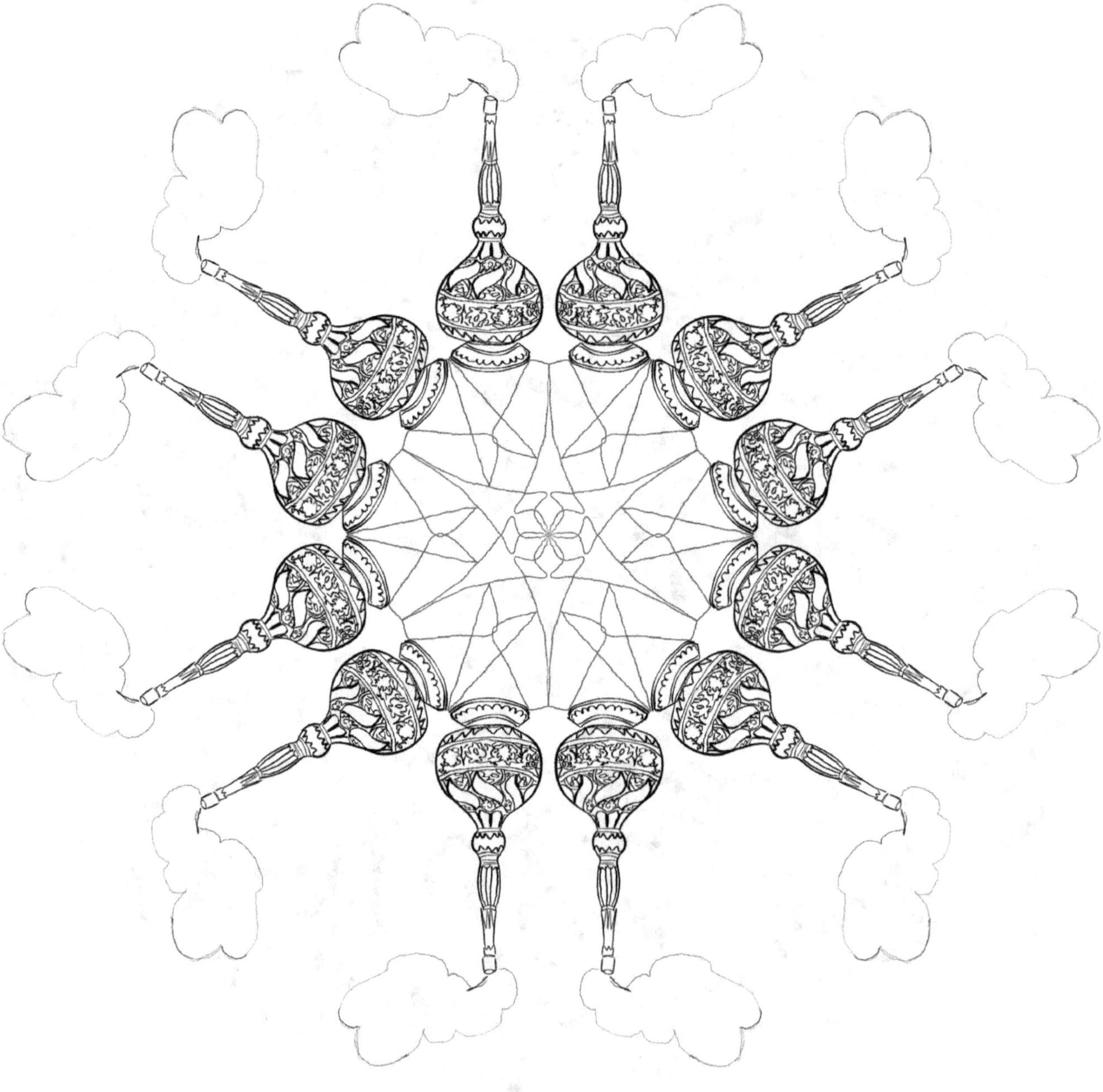

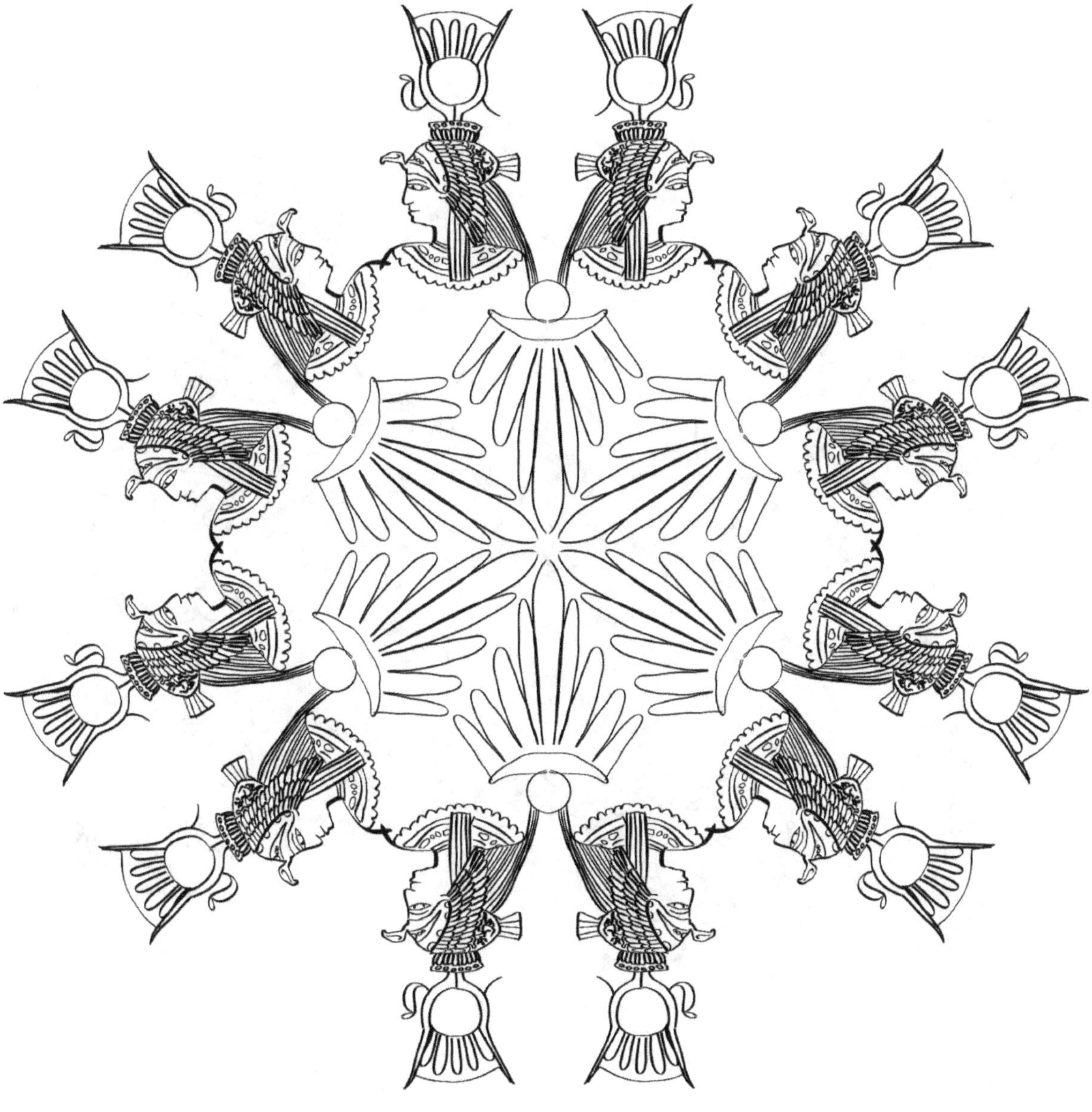

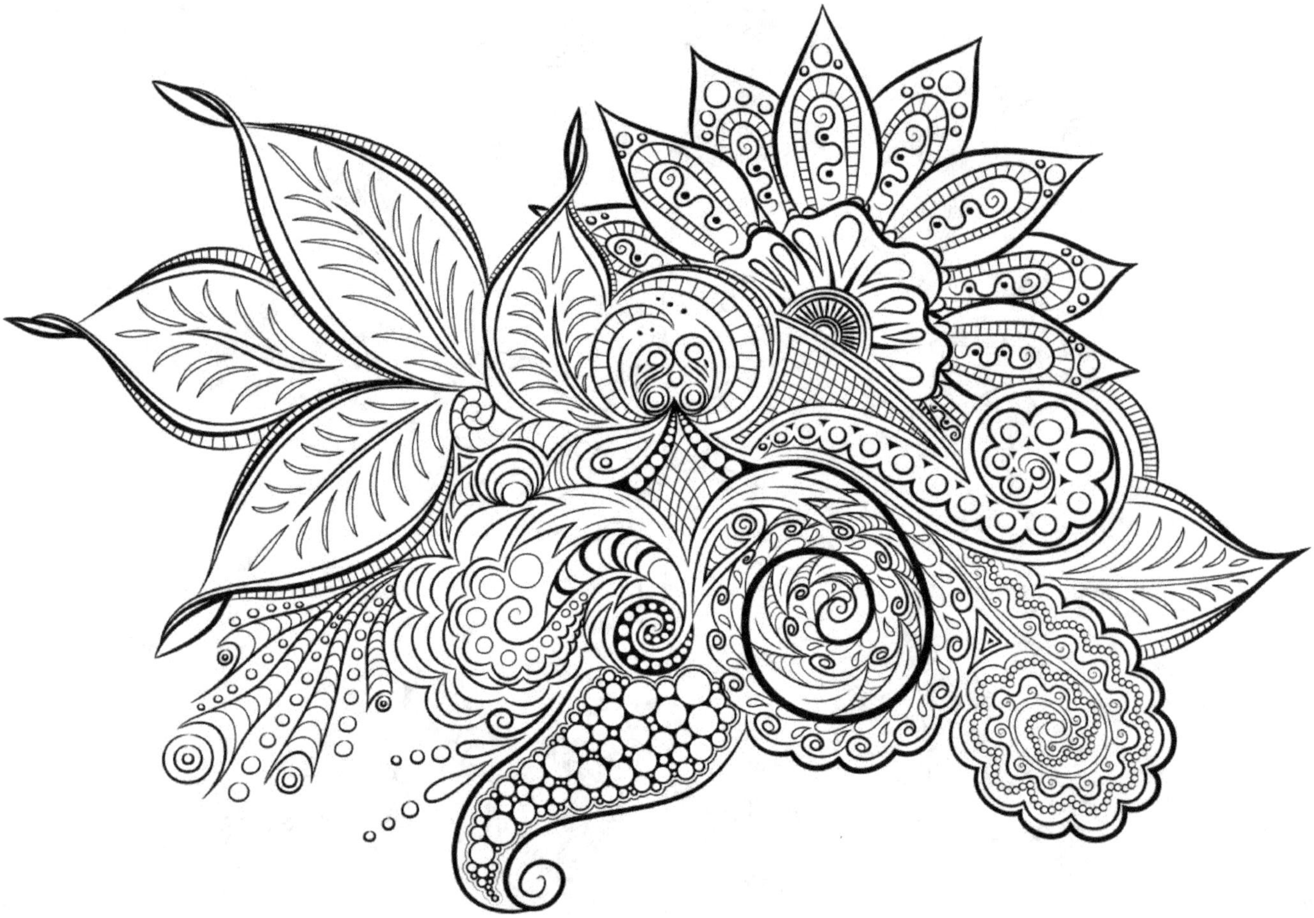

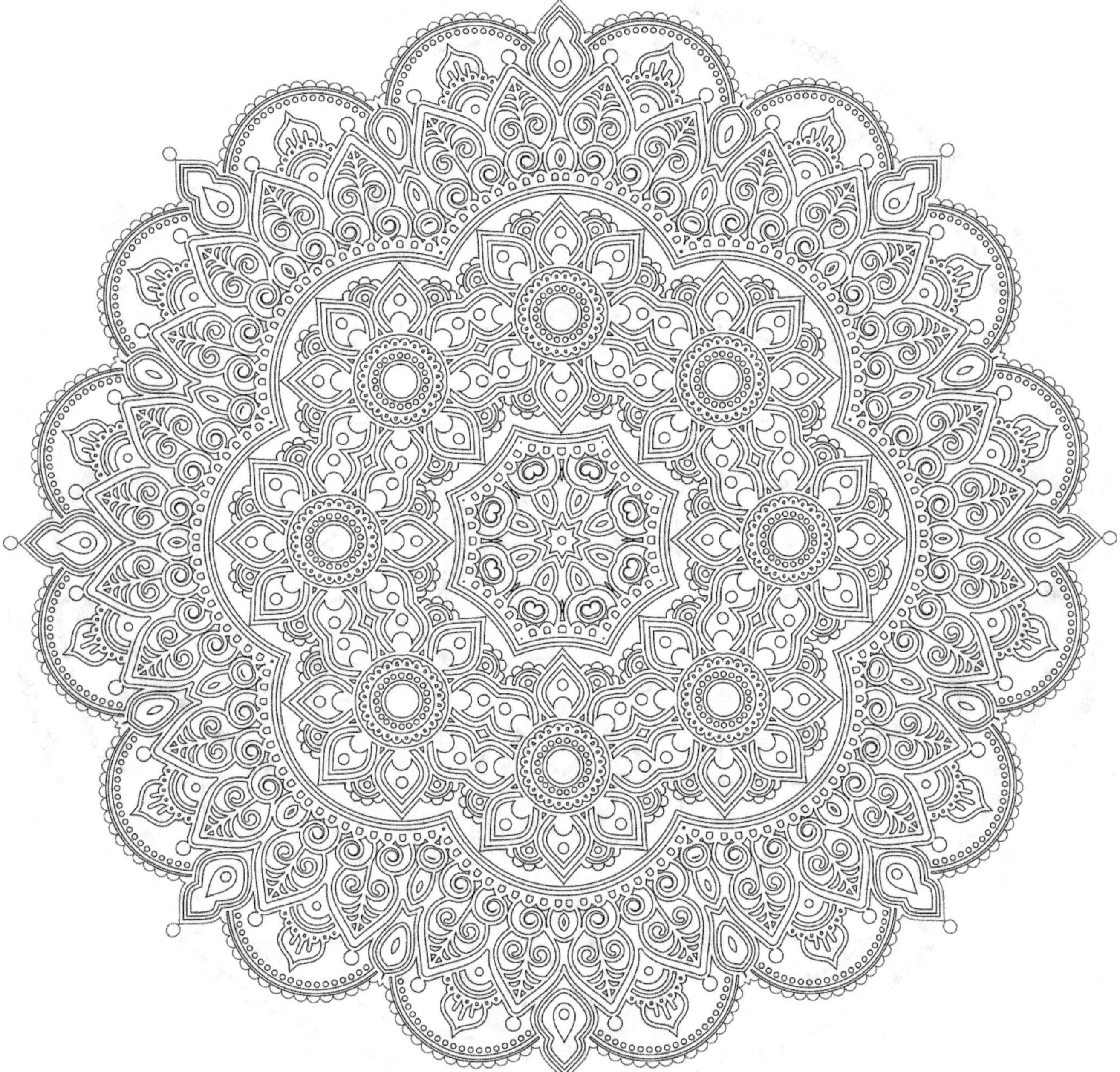

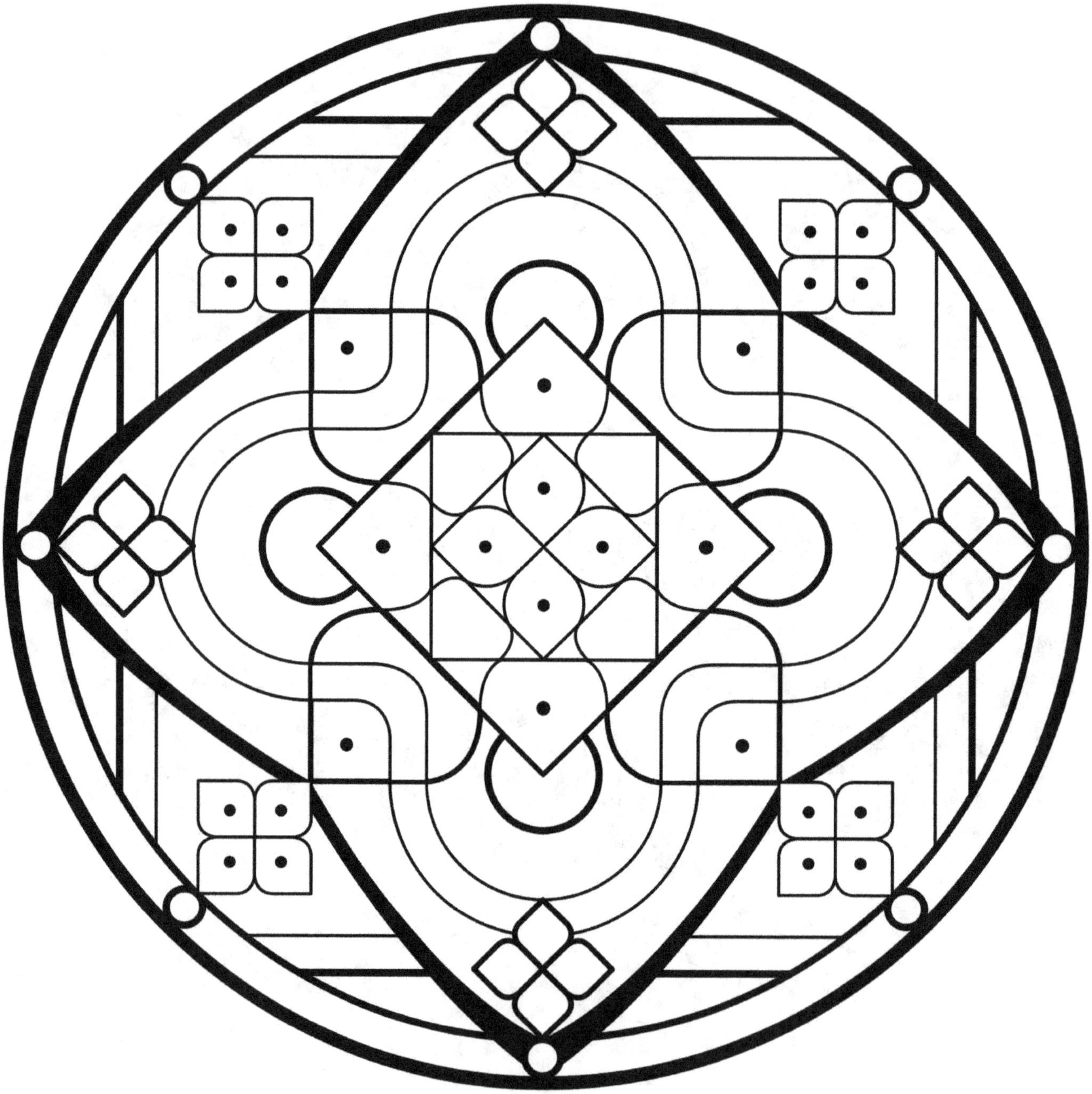

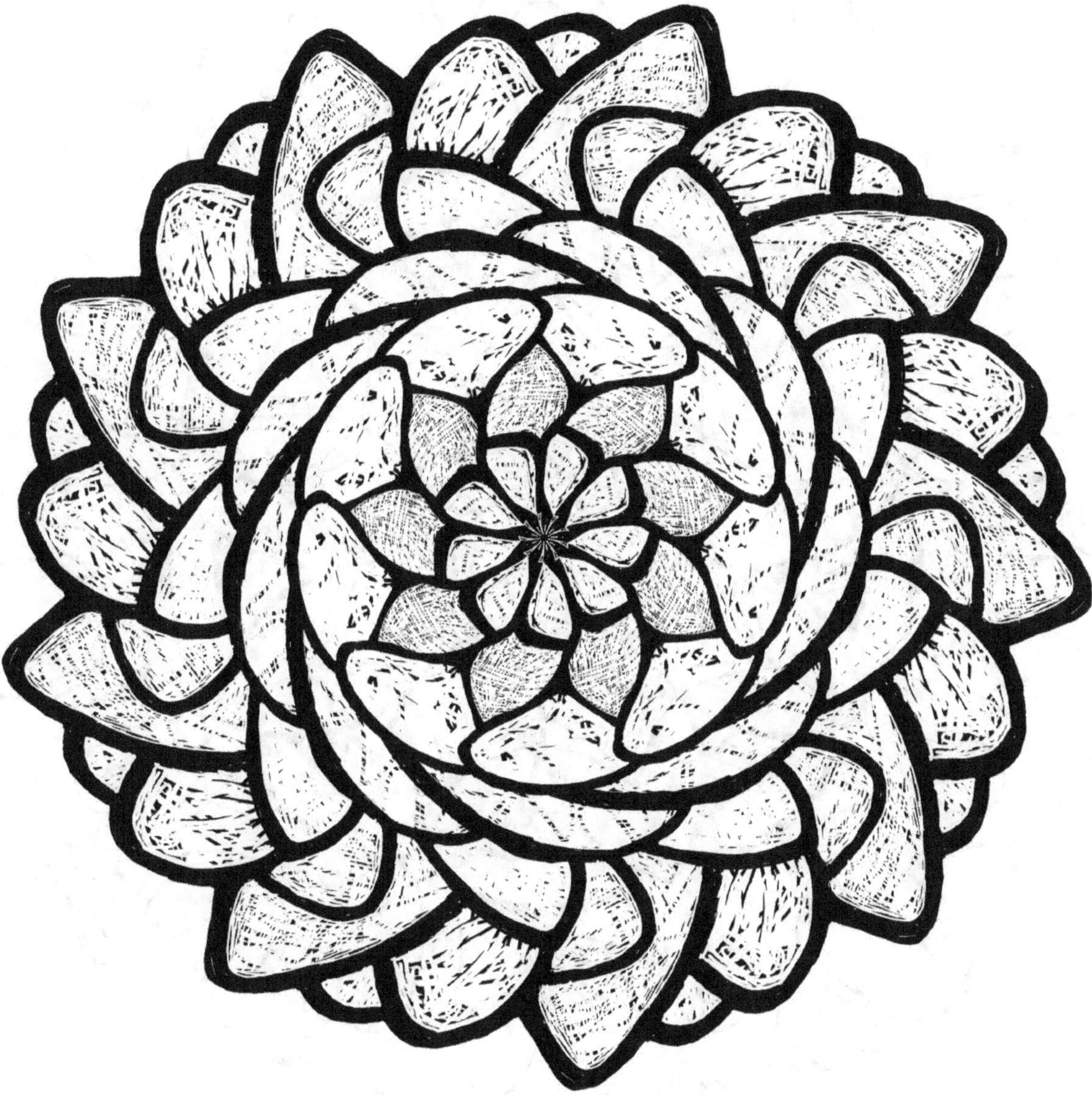

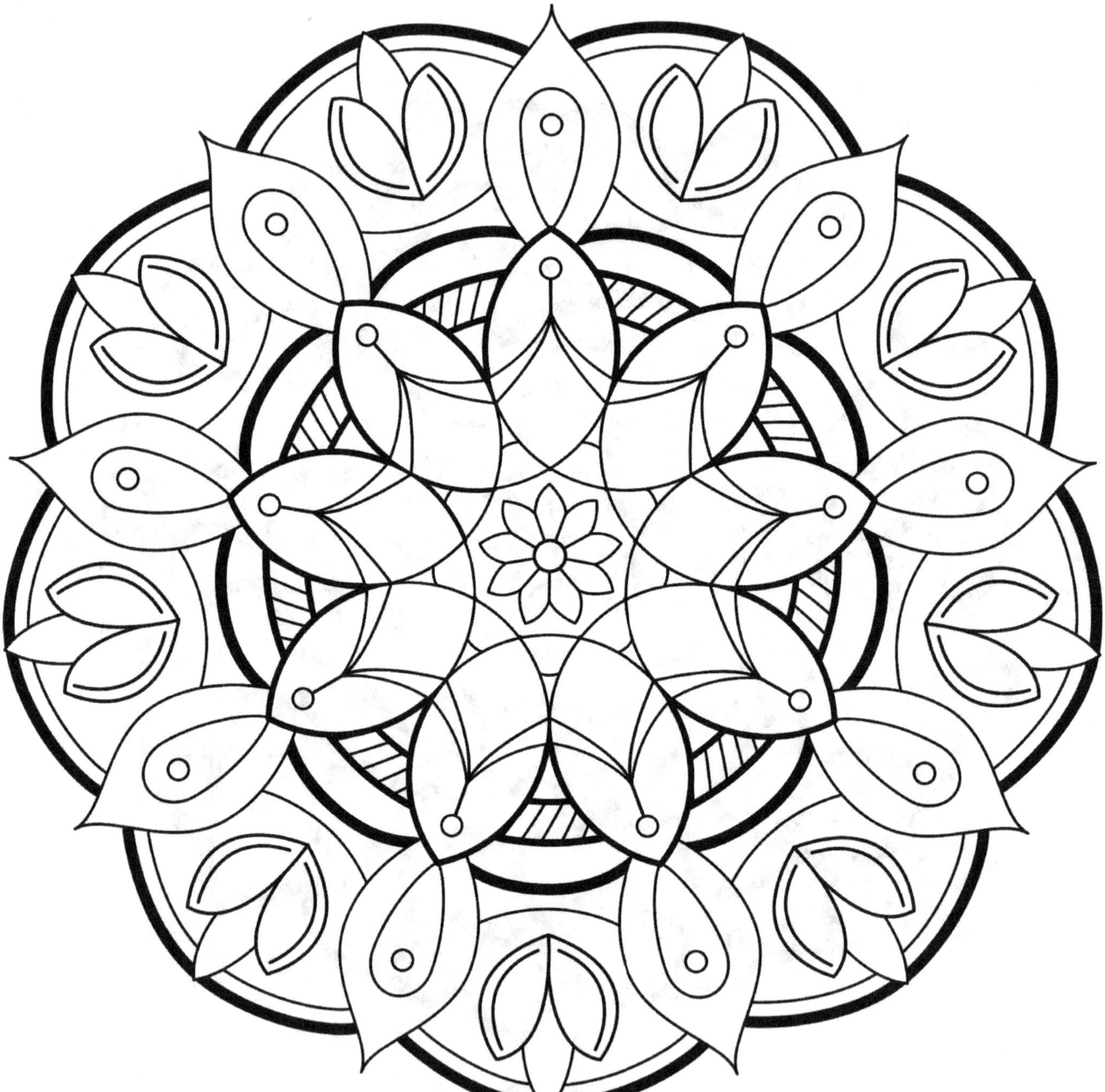

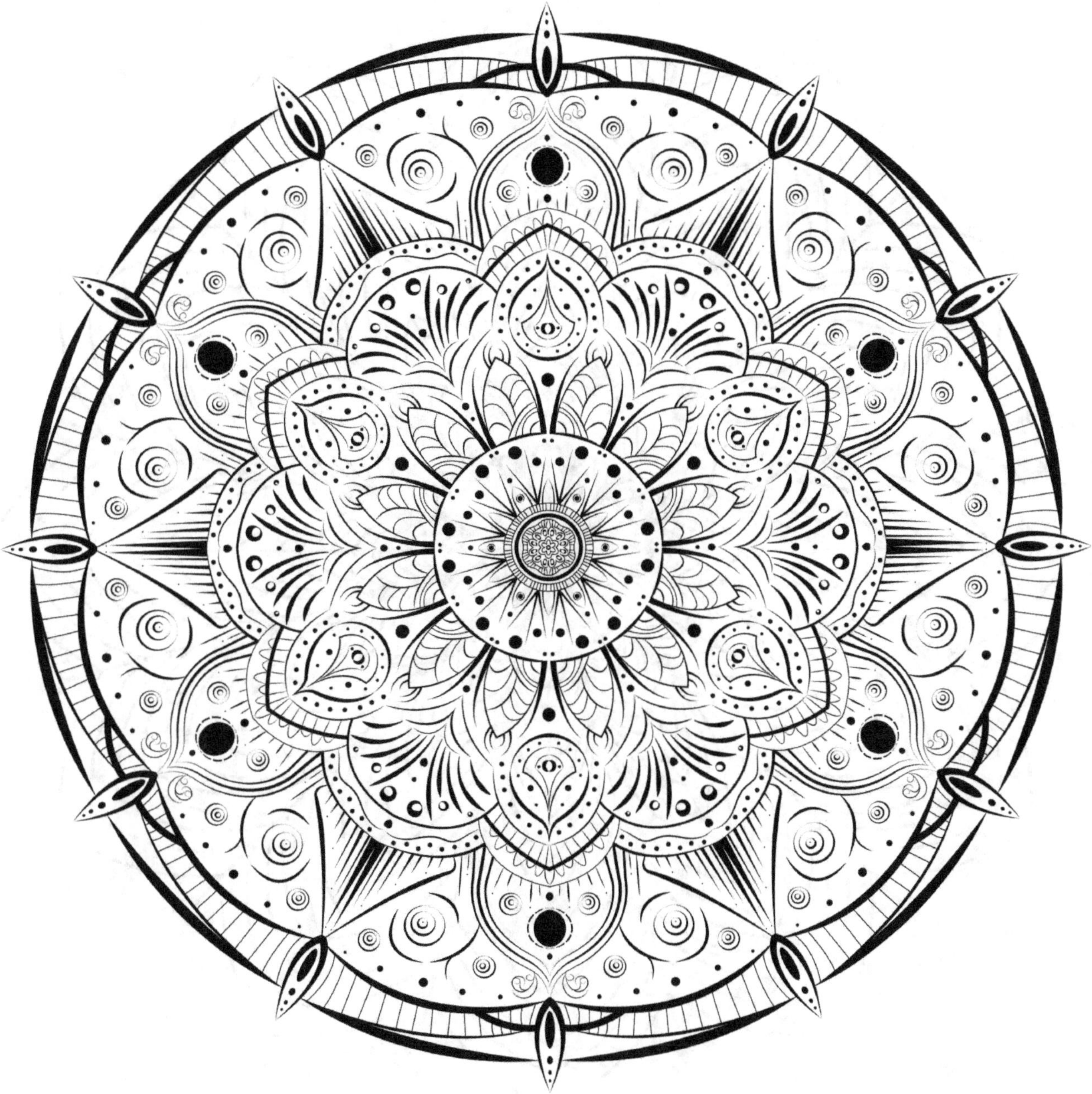

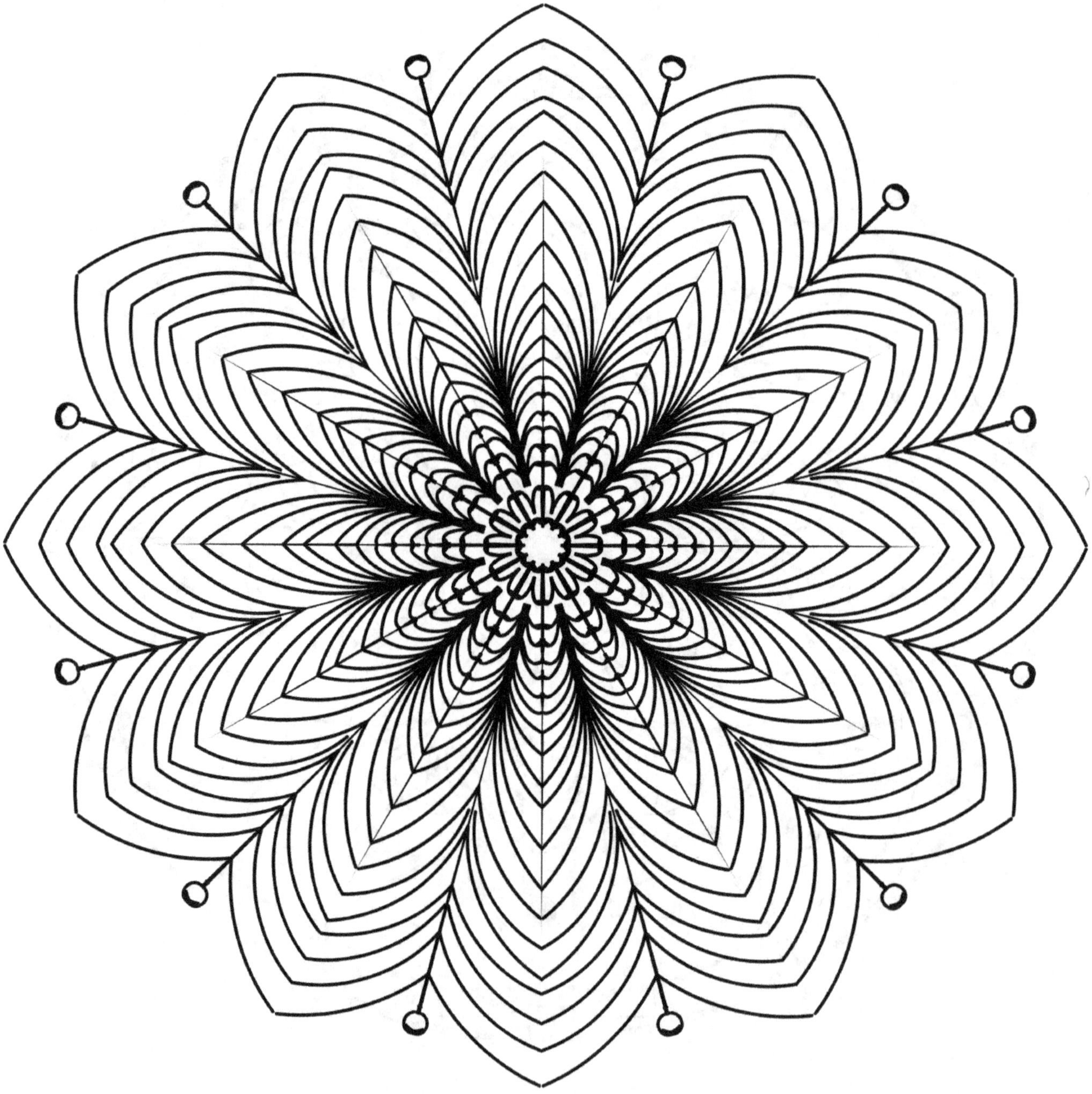

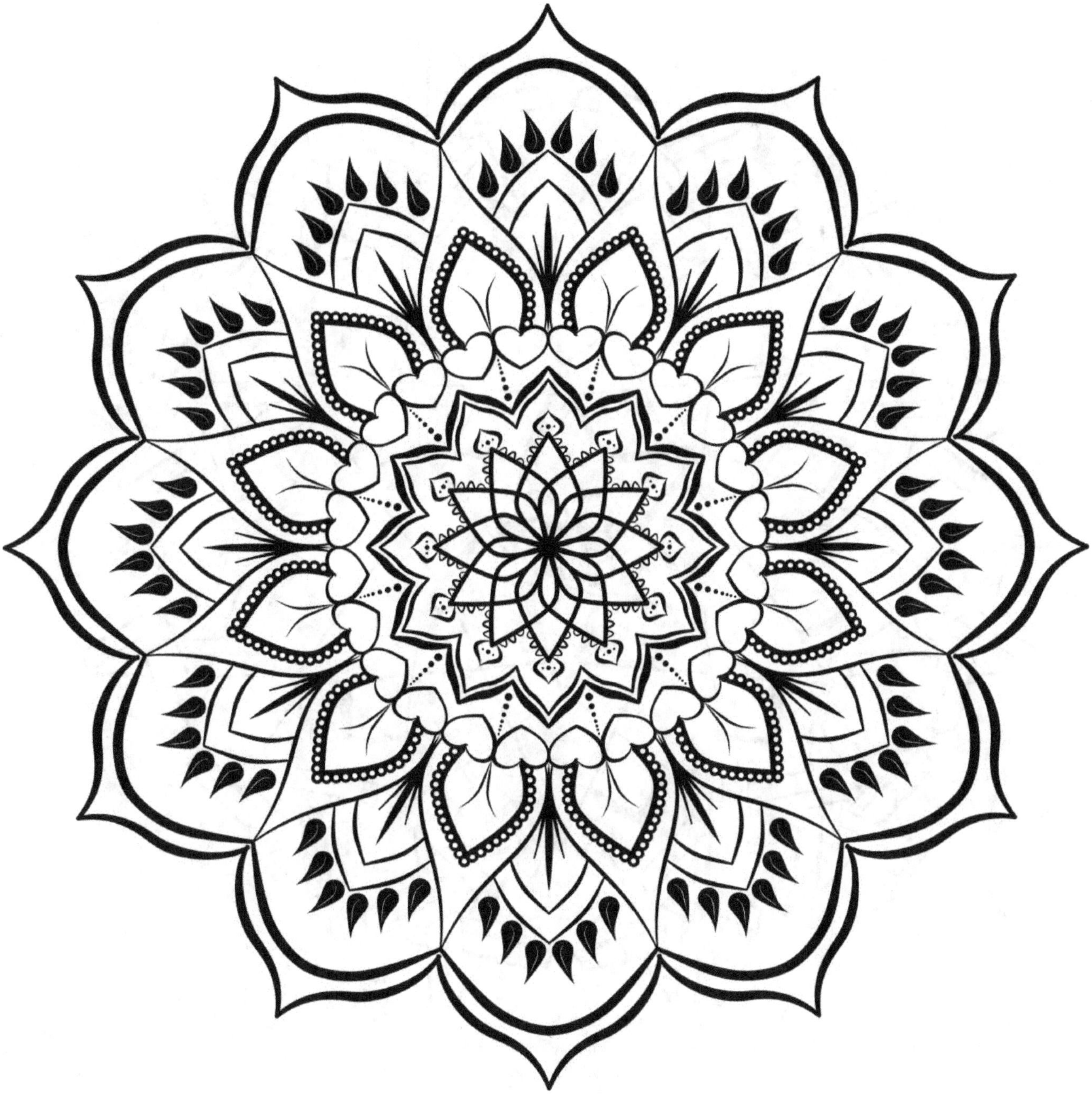

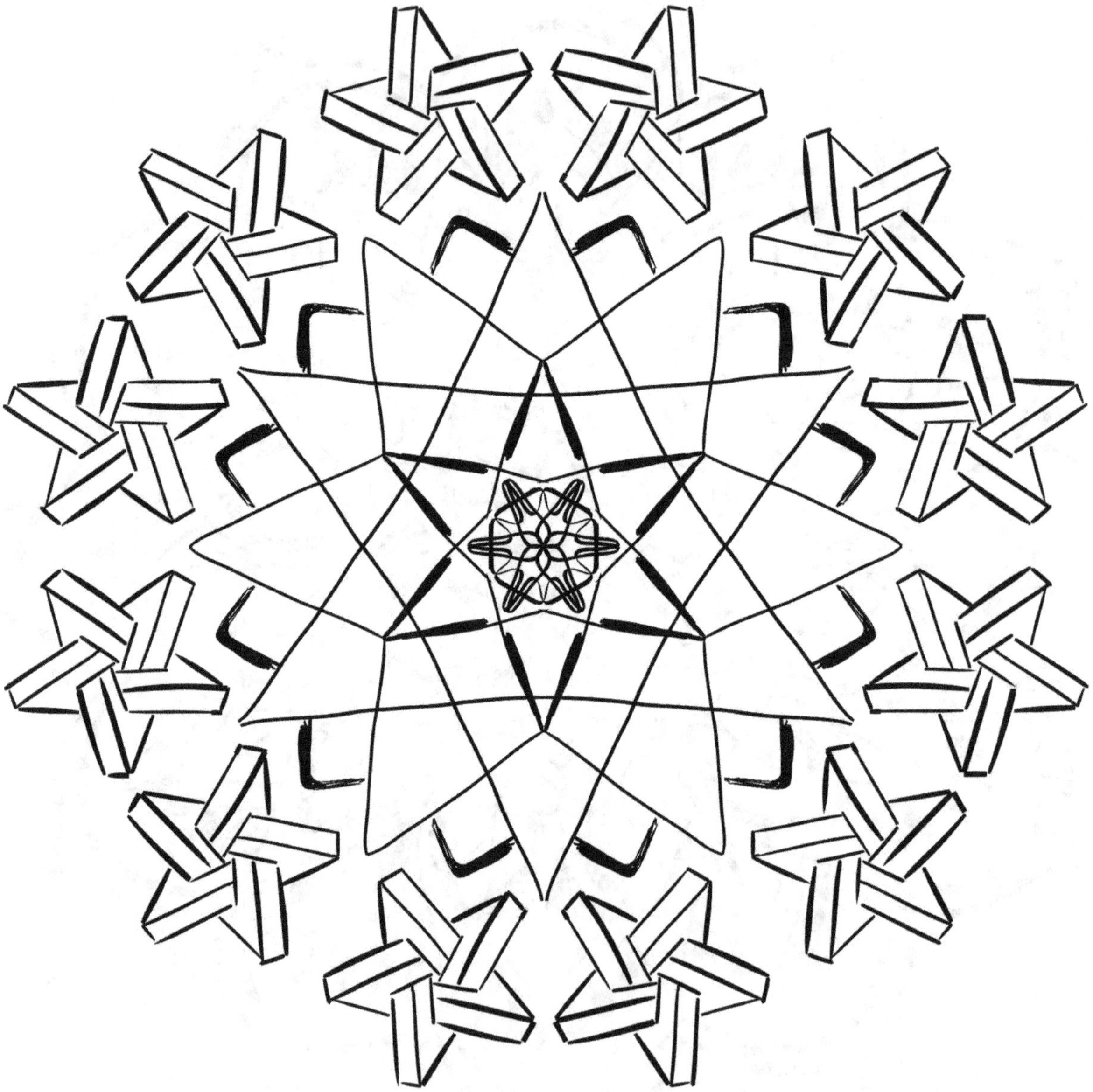

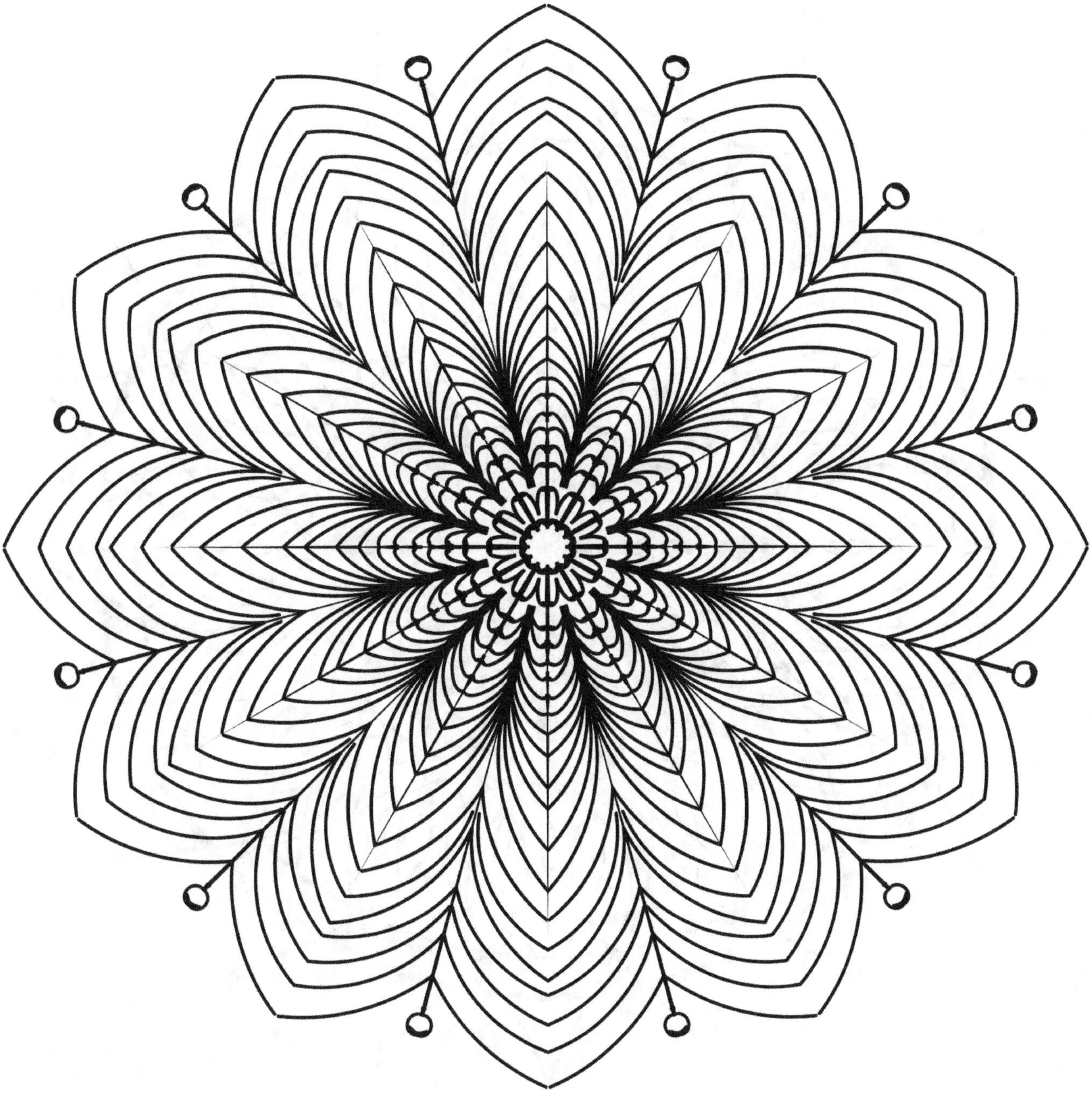

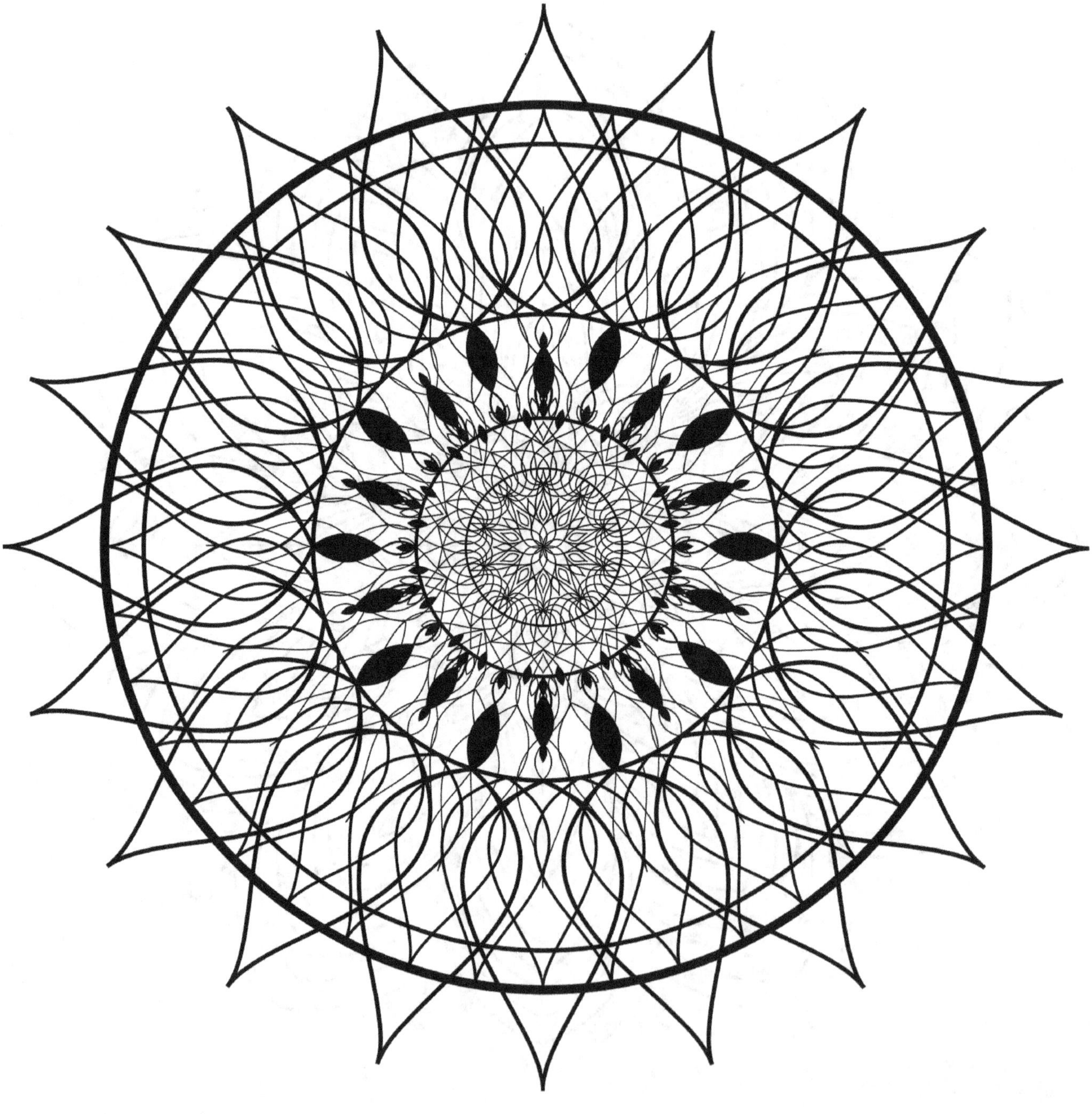

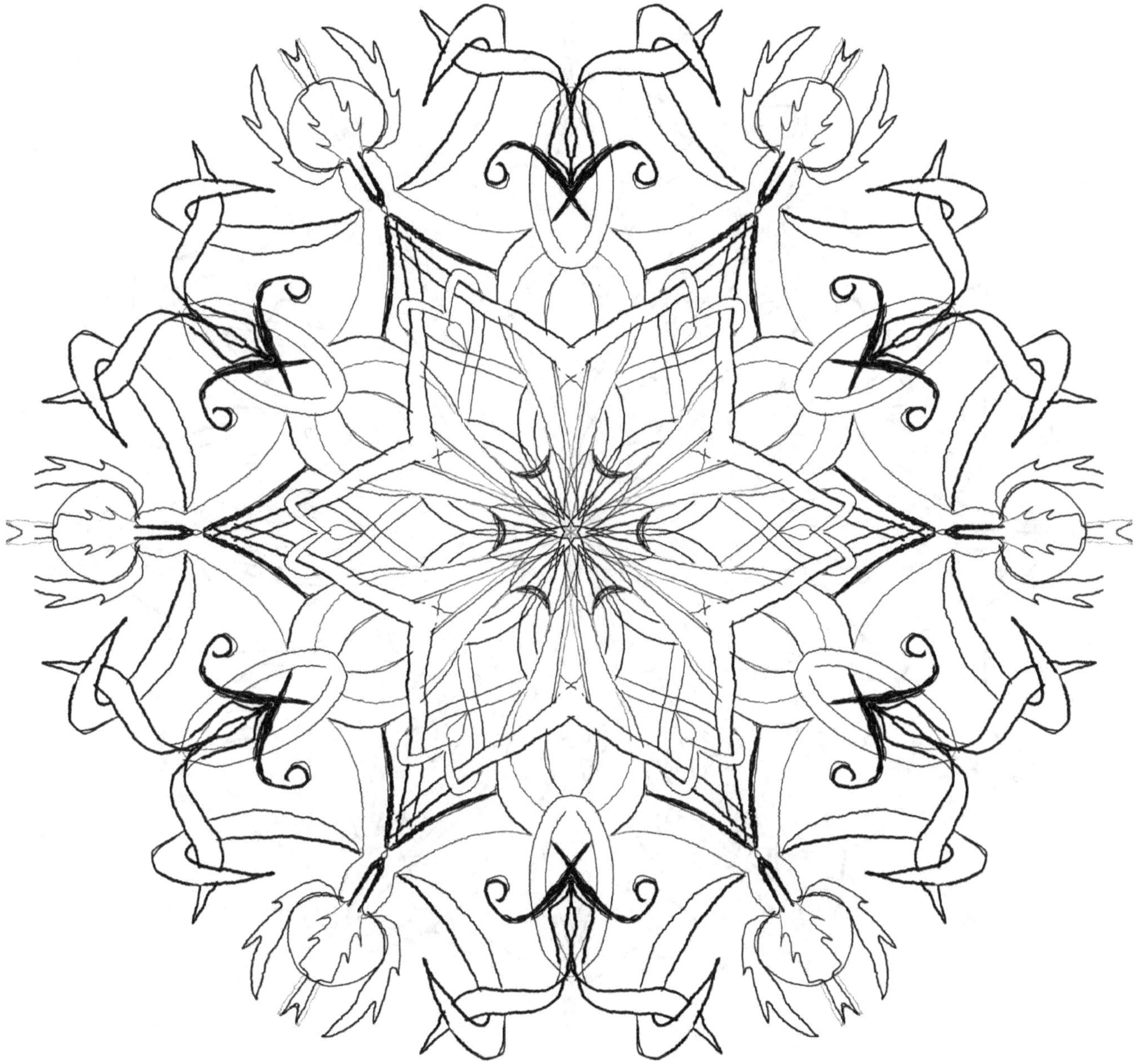

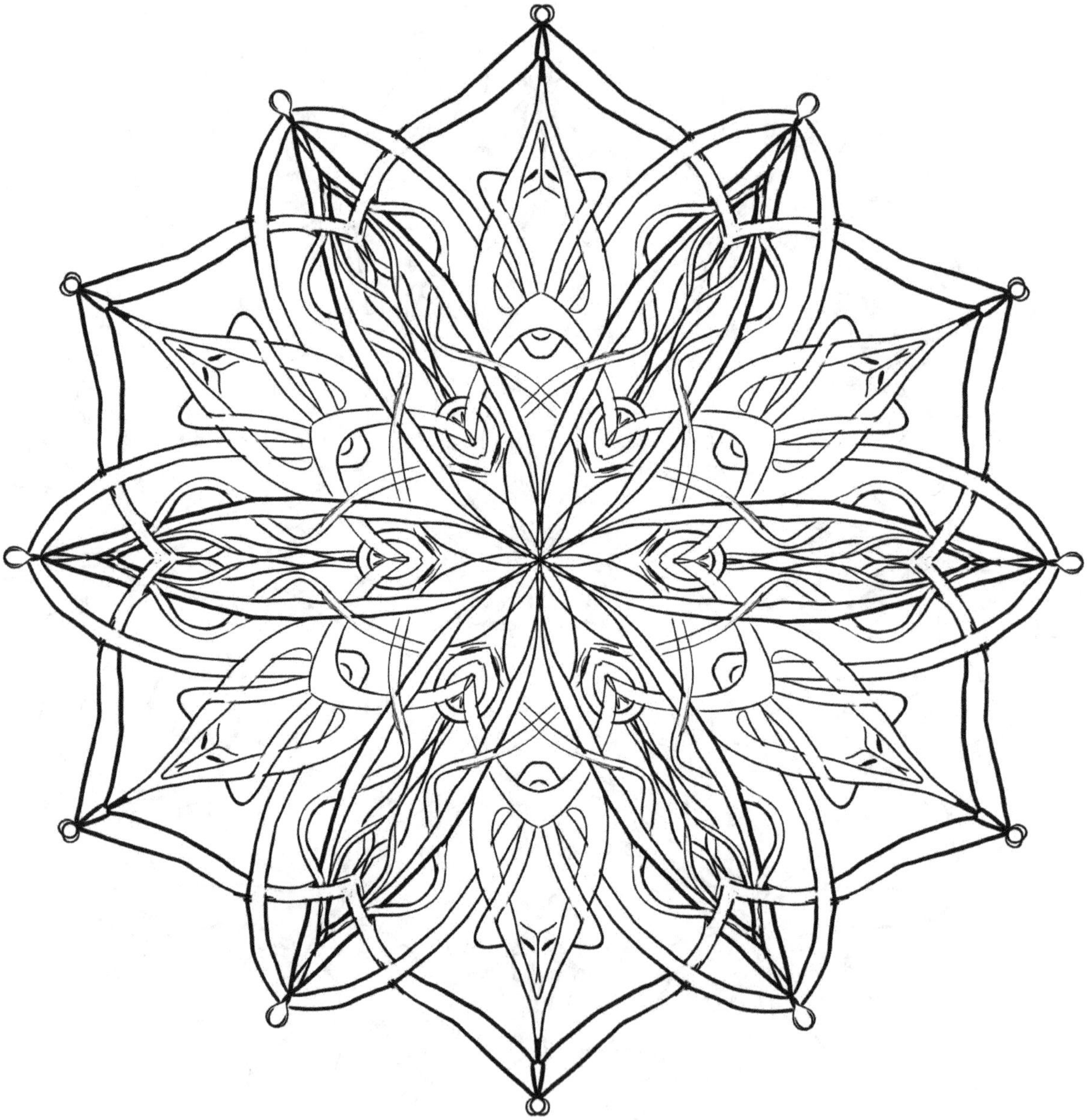

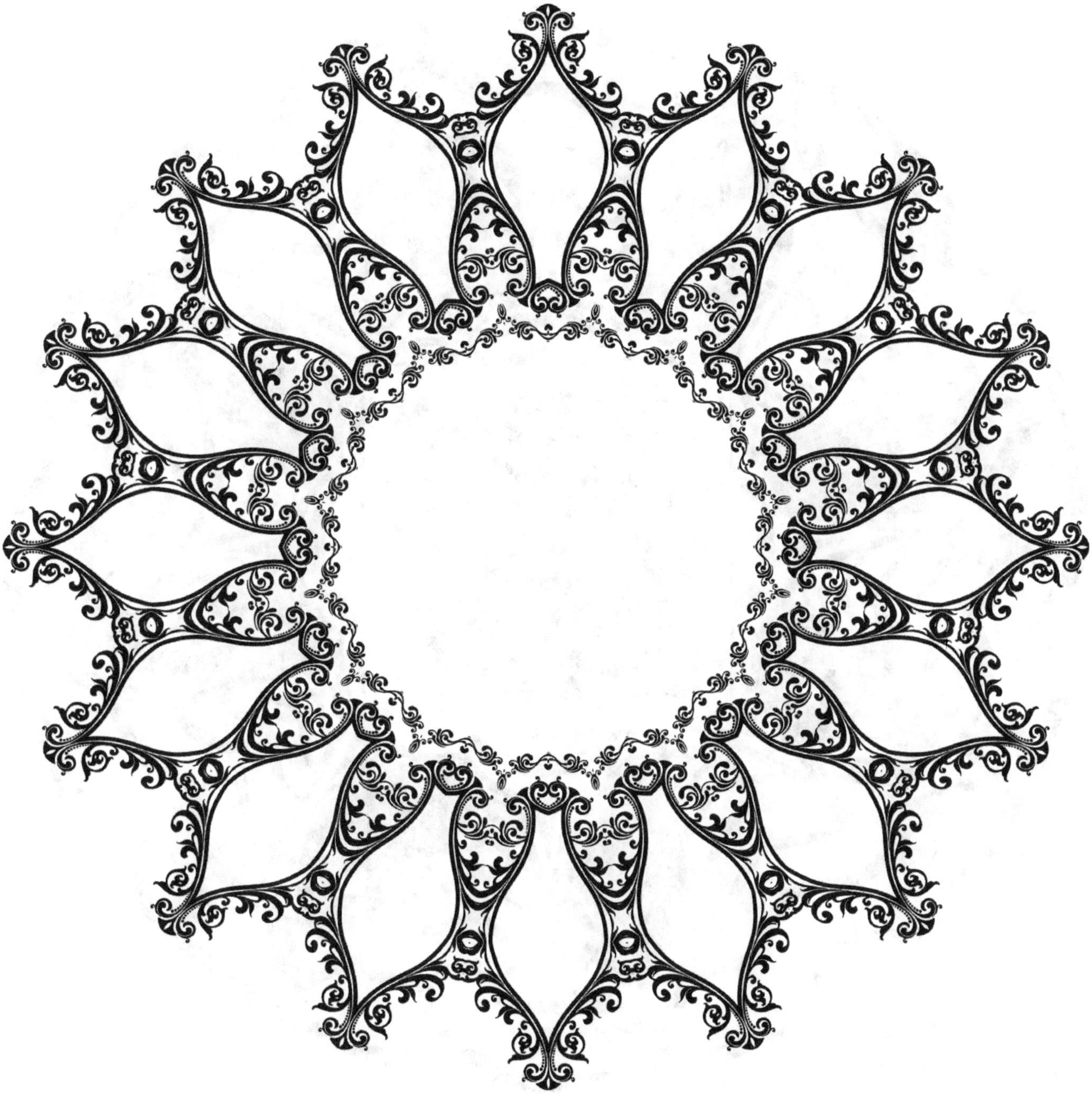

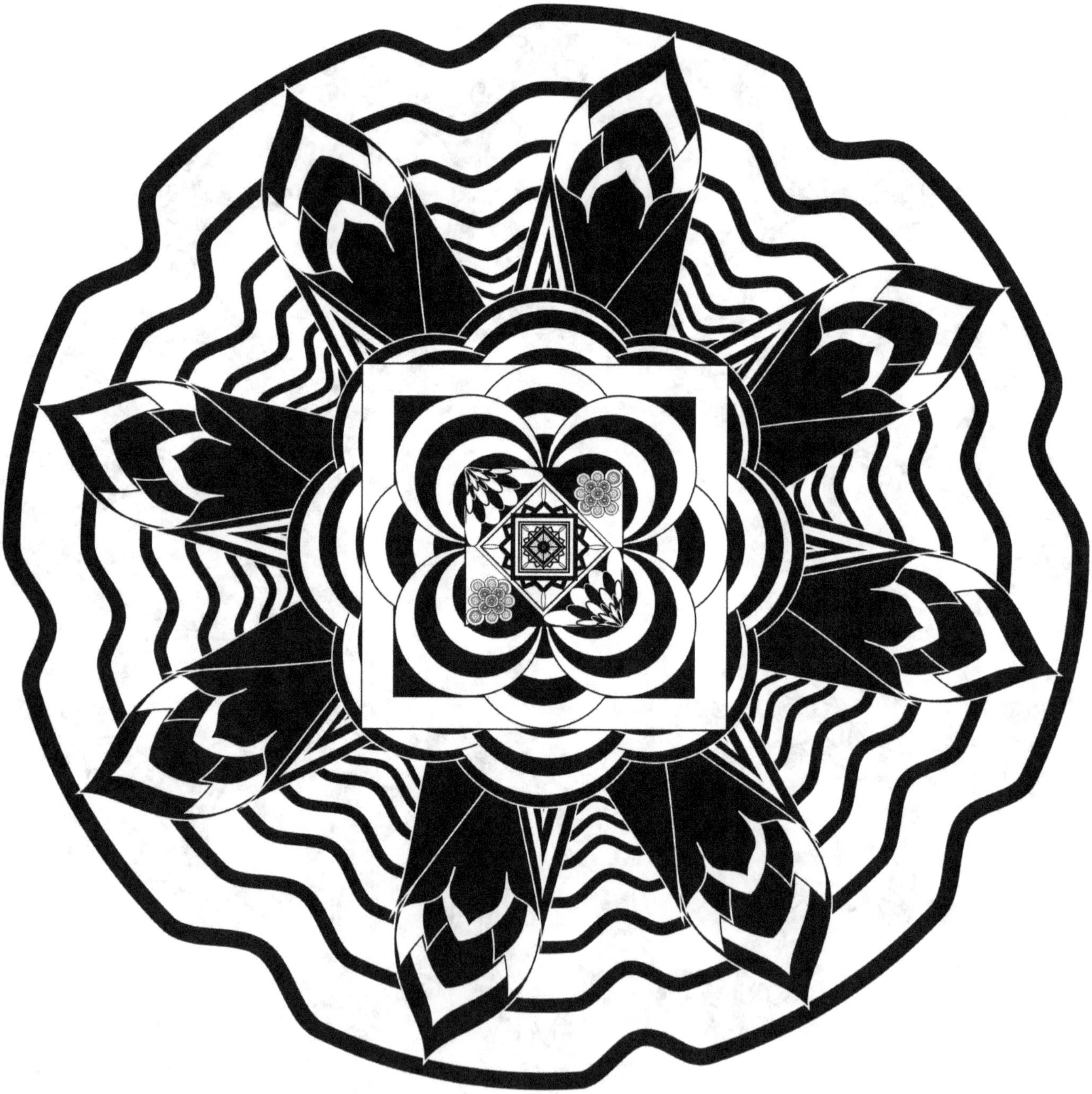

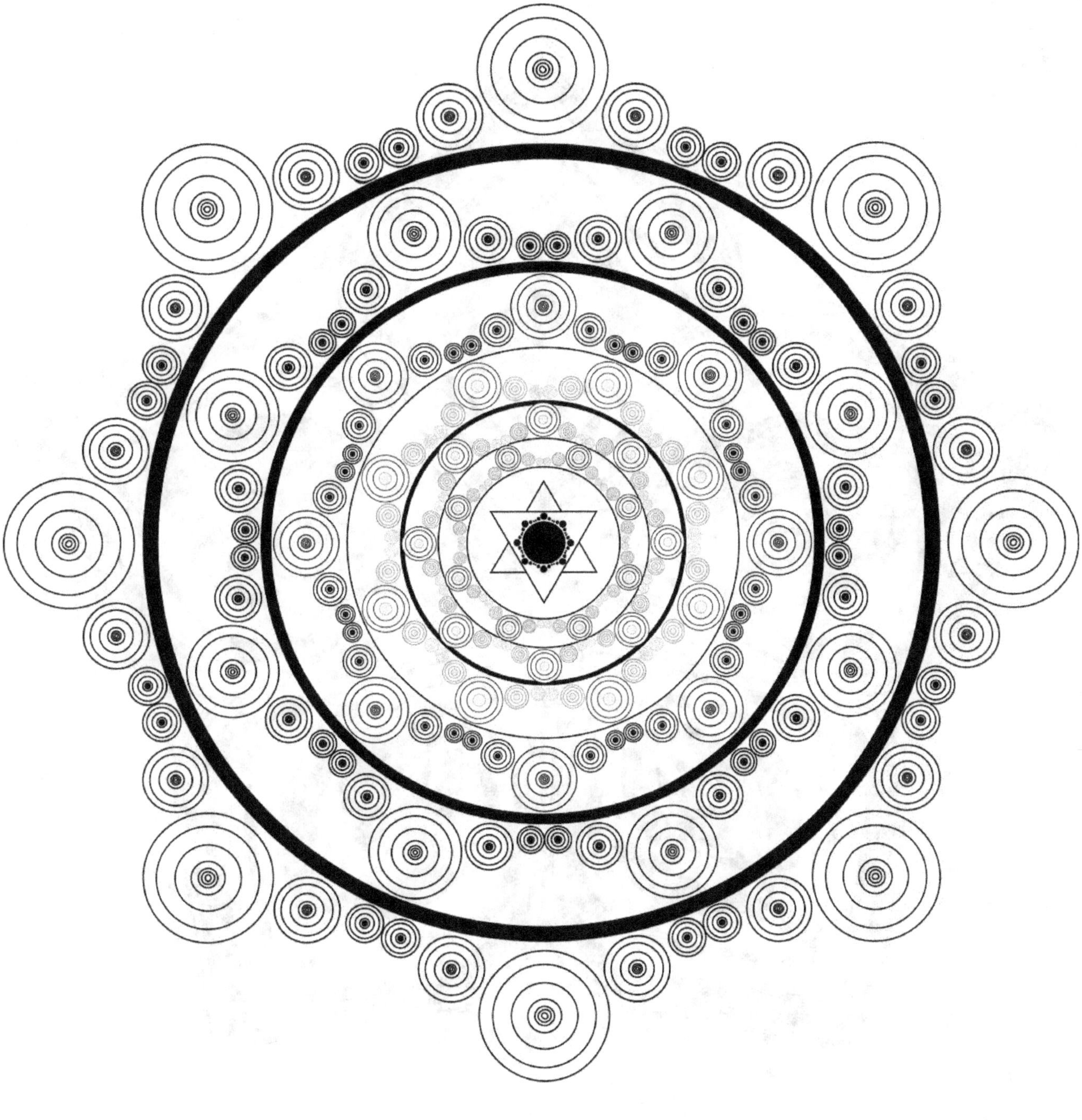

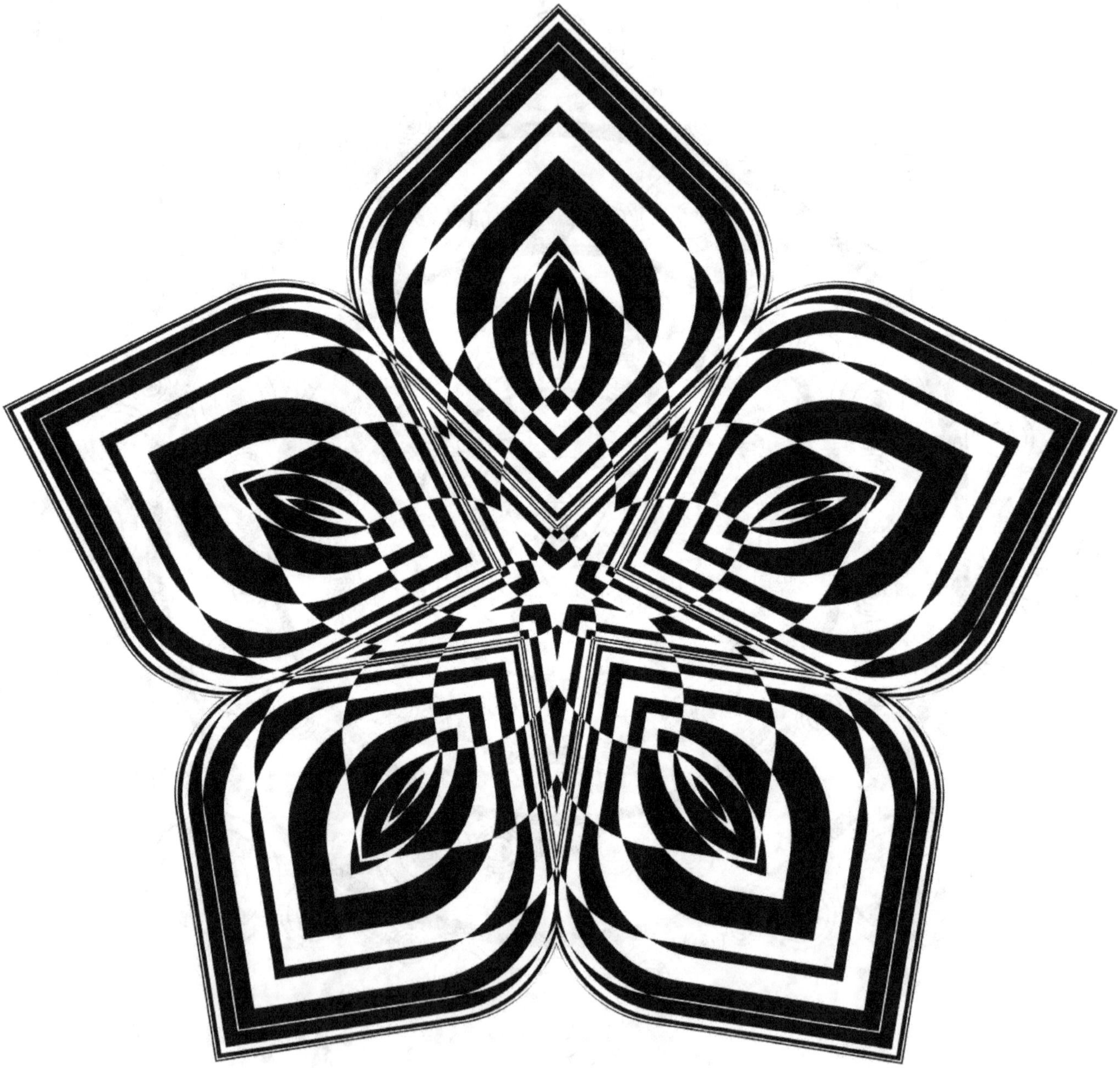

www.ingramcontent.com/pod-product-compliance
Lightning Source LLC
Chambersburg PA
CBHW081656220526
45466CB00009B/2773
9781674479446